ABRAHAM LINCOLN
IN PRINT AND PHOTOGRAPH
A Picture History from The Lilly Library

Edited by

Cecil K. Byrd and Ward W. Moore

DOVER PUBLICATIONS, INC.
Mineola, New York

To Esther and Fran

Copyright

Copyright © 1997 by Dover Publications, Inc.

All rights reserved under Pan American and International Copyright Conventions.

Published in Canada by General Publishing Company, Ltd., 30 Lesmill Road, Don Mills, Toronto, Ontario.

Published in the United Kingdom by Constable and Company, Ltd., 3 The Lanchesters, 162–164 Fulham Palace Road, London W6 9ER.

Bibliographical Note

Abraham Lincoln in Print and Photograph: A Picture History from The Lilly Library is a new work, first published by Dover Publications, Inc., in 1997.

Library of Congress Cataloging-in-Publication Data

Lilly Library (Indiana University, Bloomington)
   Abraham Lincoln in print and photograph : a picture history from The Lilly Library / edited by Cecil K. Byrd and Ward W. Moore.
      p.   cm.
   Includes index.
   ISBN 0-486-29427-7 (pbk.)
   1. Abraham Lincoln, 1809–1865—Pictorial works. 2. Abraham Lincoln, 1809–1865—Portraits. 3. Presidents—United States—Pictorial works. 4. Lilly Library (Indiana University, Bloomington)—Photographic collections. I. Byrd, Cecil K. II. Moore, Ward W. III. Title.
E457.65.L67 1997
973.7'092—dc21
[B]   96-49731
                                                 CIP

Manufactured in the United States of America
Dover Publications, Inc., 31 East 2nd Street, Mineola, N.Y. 11501

Introduction

Abraham Lincoln is extolled as "America's most revered president," the "greatest president in American history," the "unequaled man in American history." Many other superlative tributes have described the sixteenth president of the United States, and experts, polled periodically since 1948, have ranked Lincoln first among all American presidents, Washington second.

Lincoln's progress, from a humble birth in a small log cabin on the Kentucky frontier through the forested wilderness of southern Indiana and the fertile prairie of central Illinois to the White House, is a fantastic success story that has appealed to all generations. The architect of the emancipation of the slaves, he came to believe that the Declaration of Independence applied to blacks as well as whites; liberty was for all. No other public or political man of his time enunciated more strongly than he that the Federal Union was indissoluble. His tragic death—he was the first American president to be assassinated—and his sixteen-day funeral, beginning in Washington, D.C. and ending in Springfield, Illinois, represented the beginning of his apotheosis.

More has been written about this martyred leader than about any other American president. More memorials in the form of busts, paintings, plaques, and statuary have been made and erected in his memory than for any other American. Countless parks, schools, and streets are named for him, and at least thirty-six states have named towns and cities in his honor. His name has been used as a guarantor of honesty and quality in all forms of commercial enterprise, including banks, insurance companies, places of lodging, museums, and automobiles. By brief association with Lincoln, people were given a degree of fame not granted to most mortals. Certainly that was true, for example, of Grace Bedell, the young girl who suggested that Lincoln grow whiskers (see No. 99) and Elmer E. Ellsworth, who clerked in Lincoln's law office and was the first Union officer killed in the Civil War (see No. 124).

In this book we have attempted by means of photographs, lithographs, and the printed word to depict the most important events in the life of this remarkable man. The material shown, unless otherwise indicated, is in The Lilly Library of Indiana University in Bloomington, Indiana. The collection has as its nucleus the Joseph Benjamin Oakleaf Collection, acquired in 1942. Subsequent additions from a large variety of sources have greatly enlarged the original collection.

Lincoln was the first president to be photographed extensively, at least sixty-six times during his presidency. The reader should be warned that some of the photographs in this volume are crude, for photography was in its infancy in frontier Illinois during the middle decades of the nineteenth century. The first known and authenticated photograph of Lincoln dates from 1846 (No. 32). The last was taken two days after his second inauguration in 1865 (No. 189). Charles Hamilton and Lloyd Oestendorf are authorities on Lincoln photographs and their work, *Lincoln in Photographs: An Album of Every Known Pose* (Dayton: Morningside, 1985), was essential in doing research for this book. Another publication found indispensable was *The Abraham Lincoln Encyclopedia* by Mark E. Neeley, Jr. (McGraw-Hill, 1982).

We wish to thank the entire staff of The Lilly Library who generously gave assistance in the preparation of the book. We would also like to thank Margaret Zuckschwerdt and Diane Richardson of the staff of the Medical Sciences Program for their advice and help in preparation of the manuscript.

CECIL K. BYRD
WARD W. MOORE

Bloomington, Indiana

Cecil K. Byrd is Professor and Librarian Emeritus, Indiana University.
Ward W. Moore is retired Associate Dean, Indiana University School of Medicine and Emeritus Professor of Physiology and Biophysics.

Contents

	page
Introduction	v
Years in Kentucky and Indiana (Nos. 1–15)	2
Years in Illinois, to 1858 (Nos. 16–38)	11
Campaign for the U.S. Senate (Nos. 39–55)	22
First Presidential Campaign (Nos. 56–104)	31
Departure for Washington; First Administration; Civil War (Nos. 105–154)	51
Second Presidential Campaign; Second Administration (Nos. 155–190)	74
Death; Funeral; Punishment of Conspirators (Nos. 191–240)	90
Index	115

ABRAHAM LINCOLN
IN PRINT AND PHOTOGRAPH
A Picture History from The Lilly Library

Years in Kentucky and Indiana
(Nos. 1–15)

1. This monument near Hodgenville, Kentucky, is the most famous of all the state's commemorative sites. It was erected by the Lincoln Farm Association with funds obtained by popular subscription, mostly by American schoolchildren. The temple-shaped structure was designed by New York architect John Russell Pope, who also designed the National Gallery of Art and the Jefferson Memorial. It was constructed in 1909–1911 of Connecticut pink granite and Tennessee marble. Each of the fifty-six steps leading to the Lincoln Memorial building represents a year of Lincoln's life. The sixteen rosettes in the ceiling of the building symbolize Lincoln's place as the sixteenth president. President Theodore Roosevelt laid the cornerstone in 1909, and President William Howard Taft dedicated the building in 1911. In 1916, President Woodrow Wilson accepted the monument as a gift to the nation from the Lincoln Farm Association. The park in which the memorial is located is administered by the National Park Service and is officially known as the Lincoln Birthplace National Historic Site.

Abraham Lincoln was born to Thomas and Nancy Hanks Lincoln on February 12, 1809. The place of birth was a one-room log cabin located at the Sinking Spring on the south fork of Nolin Creek in Harden (now Larue) County, about three miles south of the present town of Hodgenville. Thomas Lincoln was a hardscrabble farmer who purchased three different farms in Kentucky, but lost land or money each time owing to the haphazard methods of surveying land and recording titles in the commonwealth. In disappointment and frustration, and perhaps because of his antislavery attitude and the presence of slavery in Kentucky, he moved to Indiana in the fall of 1816.

Abraham thus spent the first seven years of his life in Kentucky. As an adult he recalled that he and his sister were sent for short periods in the fall of 1815 to "A.B.C. schools" kept by Zachariah Riney and Caleb Hazel. His parents and later his stepmother encouraged him to learn to read and gain knowledge.

2. The Lincoln Memorial building near Hodgenville contains this small (sixteen by eighteen feet) one-room log cabin, built of native hardwood logs, chinked with clay, and heated by a stone-lined fireplace. It has an obscure history, and extensive research has failed to prove that it is indisputably Lincoln's birth cabin. It was moved to a site near the Sinking Spring in 1894, dismantled and reerected for exhibit in many cities. The Lincoln Farm Association bought the cabin in 1906 and placed it in the Memorial Building.

4. When Abraham Lincoln was two years of age, in the spring of 1811, he and his father, his mother, and his four-year-old sister, Sarah, moved to a more fertile farm of some 230 acres located near the banks of Knob Creek, about eight miles north and east of his birthplace. They built a small log cabin and lived there until the fall of 1816. Abraham and Sarah attended school nearby. Their younger brother, Thomas Jr., was born here but died in infancy. Lincoln's earliest recollection was of "the Knob Creek Place." The cabin in this photograph presumably stands on the site of the original Lincoln cabin. The logs were taken from another old cabin and recut to the size of the original cabin in 1931. It is listed in the National Register of Historic Places and is administered by the Commonwealth of Kentucky.

3. This bronze statue of a seated Lincoln graces the Hodgenville public square. The sculptor, Adolph A. Weinman, and the president's son Robert Todd Lincoln were among the many honored guests attending the unveiling ceremony on May 31, 1909. A small replica is in the Lincoln Tomb in Springfield, Illinois. Although Hodgenville was not created until 1818, two years after the Lincolns left Kentucky for Indiana, the town has publicized its propinquity to Lincoln's birthplace by placing the president's name to a number of commercial establishments, including a bank, a motel, a museum, and an antiques mall.

5. The Lincoln family arrived in Indiana in mid-December 1816, the same week that Indiana was admitted to the Union as the nineteenth state. After ferrying across the Ohio River from Kentucky to near the mouth of the Anderson River at Troy in Perry County (the Lincoln Ferry Park, now in Spencer County, marks the site of their arrival), they followed a rough wagon road northwest for about eight miles and literally hacked their way through the forest for another four miles to the spot to which Thomas Lincoln had laid claim. There they erected a log cabin. In August 1817 Thomas Lincoln purchased 120 acres east of the village of Gentryville, and the Lincolns lived there in what is now Spencer County until they moved to Illinois. The replicated cabin in this photograph stands a few feet north of the original site; it and its outbuildings are part of a living historical farm created by the National Park Service at the Lincoln Boyhood National Memorial near Lincoln City, Indiana.

Abraham Lincoln spent fourteen formative years in Indiana, from 1816 to 1830. Except for a sum-book leaf (see No. 7), no contemporary written documentation exists for this period. Two autobiographical sketches Lincoln prepared for political friends pushing him toward the presidency are the primary sources of information. One was written for Jesse W. Fell of Bloomington, Illinois, on December 20, 1859, for use in Republican newspapers before his nomination. The other, written in the third person in June 1860, was for John L. Scripps, who was preparing a campaign biography. The latter, longer and more informative, states that:

> A. [Abraham] though very young, was large of his age, and had an axe put into his hands at once; and from that till within his twentythird year, he was almost constantly handling that most useful instrument—less of course, in plowing and harvesting seasons. . . . In the autumn of 1818 his mother died; and a year afterwards his father married Mrs. Sally [Sarah] Johnston, at Elizabeth-Town, Ky—a widow, with three children of her first marriage. She proved a good and kind mother to A. . . . While here A. went to A.B.C. schools by littles, kept successively by Andrew Crawford, —— Sweeney [James Swaney], and Azel W. Dorsey. He does not remember any other . . . A. now thinks that the agregate of all his schooling did not amount to one year. . . . What he has in the way of education, he has picked up. . . . When he was nineteen, still residing in Indiana, he made his first trip upon a flat-boat to New-Orleans. He was a hired hand merely; and he and a son [Allen Gentry] of the owner [James Gentry], without other assistance, made the trip. The nature of part of the cargo-load, as it was called —made it necessary for them to linger and trade along the Sugar coast [Louisiana]—and one night they were attacked by seven negroes with intent to kill and rob them. They were hurt some in the melee, but succeeded in driving the negroes from the boat and then "cut cable" "weighed anchor" and left.

Later recollections given to Lincoln's last law partner and biographer, William H. Herndon, by relatives and friends who knew him as a youth are highly suspect and contradictory. But we are told and generally accept that Lincoln's father permitted him to be hired by others when work was slack on the Lincoln farm. In 1827, he worked for James Taylor for nine months as a farmhand and helper on a ferry at the confluence of the Anderson and Ohio rivers. In 1829 he worked in the store of James Gentry at a settlement later named Gentryville. Most of the latter-day informants agree that the youthful Lincoln read many borrowed books; was, like his father, a good storyteller; and had a talent for mimicry. Perhaps it can be said that his boyhood and teenage years in Indiana were typical for the time and place, exceptional only in that he read more than was normal for a frontier Indiana youth, eschewed alcohol and tobacco, and was not fond of hunting. The youthful Lincoln was encouraged to read and to learn by his mother (who was illiterate) and later by his stepmother.

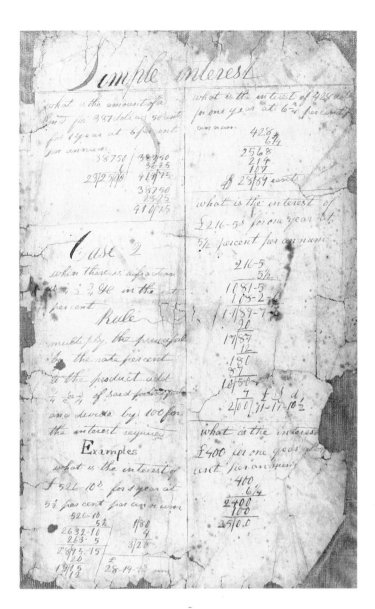

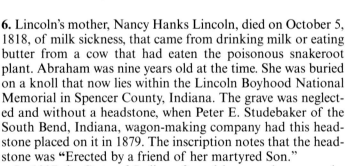

6. Lincoln's mother, Nancy Hanks Lincoln, died on October 5, 1818, of milk sickness, that came from drinking milk or eating butter from a cow that had eaten the poisonous snakeroot plant. Abraham was nine years old at the time. She was buried on a knoll that now lies within the Lincoln Boyhood National Memorial in Spencer County, Indiana. The grave was neglected and without a headstone, when Peter E. Studebaker of the South Bend, Indiana, wagon-making company had this headstone placed on it in 1879. The inscription notes that the headstone was "Erected by a friend of her martyred Son."

In 1907 the State of Indiana fenced in several acres encircling the grave and named it the Nancy Hanks Lincoln Park. The park gradually evolved into a memorial to Abraham. Beginning in 1926, through the recommendations of the Indiana Lincoln Union, the state bought the land and transformed the area around the original Lincoln cabin site. In 1962 the park became part of the Lincoln Boyhood National Memorial, administered by the National Park Service.

Lincoln lost two beloved family members in Indiana. In addition to his mother, his only sister, Sarah Lincoln Grigsby, died in childbirth on January 20, 1828, age twenty-one, and is buried along with her stillborn baby in the Little Pigeon Creek Baptist Church Cemetery, located about two miles south of her mother's grave.

7. This leaf from a booklet Lincoln made to hold his arithmetic exercises from 1824 to 1826 represents the earliest known example of his penmanship. William H. Herndon, law partner and biographer of Lincoln, obtained the sum-book from Lincoln's stepmother, Sarah Bush Johnston Lincoln, in September 1865 on a visit to her Coles County, Illinois, home after Lincoln's death. Ten sheets are known to survive and are reproduced in Volume 1 of *The Collected Works of Abraham Lincoln*. The Lilly Library leaf was a gift from Foreman M. Lebold in 1949.

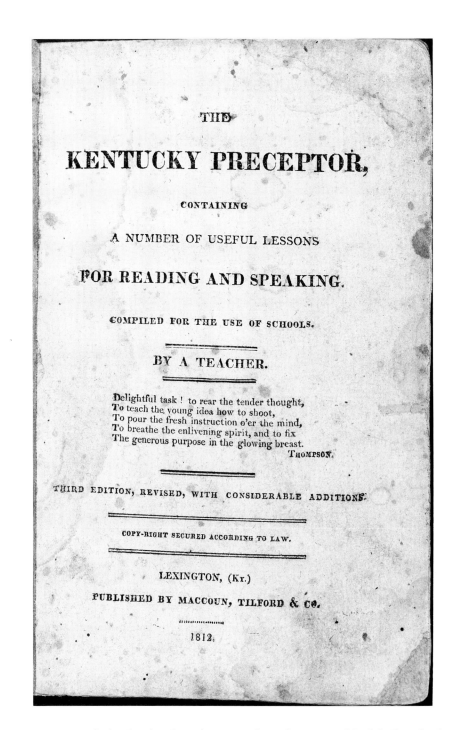

THE

KENTUCKY PRECEPTOR,

CONTAINING

A NUMBER OF USEFUL LESSONS

FOR READING AND SPEAKING.

COMPILED FOR THE USE OF SCHOOLS.

BY A TEACHER.

Delightful task ! to rear the tender thought,
To teach the young idea how to shoot,
To pour the fresh instruction o'er the mind,
To breathe the enlivening spirit, and to fix
The generous purpose in the glowing breast.
THOMPSON.

THIRD EDITION, REVISED, WITH CONSIDERABLE ADDITIONS.

COPY-RIGHT SECURED ACCORDING TO LAW.

LEXINGTON, (Ky.)
PUBLISHED BY MACCOUN, TILFORD & Co.

1812.

8. *The Kentucky Preceptor* was one of the books that the youthful Lincoln reportedly borrowed from a neighbor in southern Indiana. Lincoln biographer William H. Herndon interviewed Elizabeth Crawford, wife of Josiah Crawford, owner of the book, on September 16, 1865, and Mrs. Crawford gave the book to Herndon. Later, Herndon inscribed the book on the front flyleaf: "To Mr. Jno. E. Remington. This book was given to me by Mrs. Elizabeth Crawford of the State of Indiana, who lived near Mr. Lincoln's old home in Indiana. As I understand knew Mr. Lincoln well. This book is the one out of which Mr. Lincoln learned his speeches as I was told by Mrs. Crawford and which I have good reason to believe to be true. W. H. Herndon." On the free portion of the back end sheet the name of Josiah Crawford and the date 1819 are written.

The book contains essays selected from various sources relating to industry, magnanimity, remorse of conscience, Columbus, Demosthenes, the Scriptures as a rule of life, credulity, and liberty and slavery. Thomas Jefferson's 1801 Inaugural Address is also included.

The book eventually entered the collection of Oliver R. Barrett. It was sold at public auction at the Parke-Bernet Galleries in 1952 and purchased by the late Foreman M. Lebold of Chicago. Lebold gave the book to Indiana University in 1953.

9. This bronze statue, ten feet tall above its five-foot base, depicts Lincoln as a teenage, barefoot Hoosier carrying a book. It was sculptured in 1962 by David K. Rubins of Indianapolis, a long-time faculty member of the Herron School of Art and Indiana University. It is now in its third location: on Government Place between two Indiana Government Center buildings west of the Statehouse in Indianapolis.

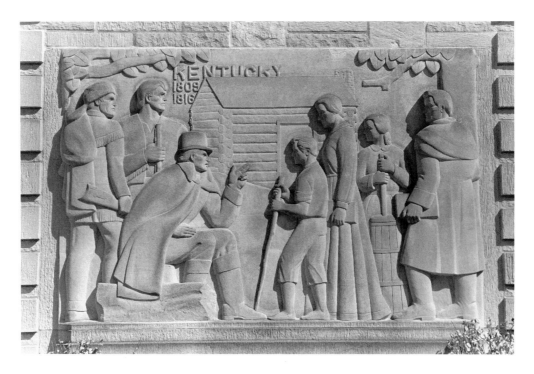

10. The Visitor Center of the Lincoln Boyhood National Memorial in Spencer County, Indiana, was designed by Elmer Harland "E. H." Daniels. Daniels also sculptured five large panels of limestone (Nos. 10–13 and 240), each depicting a major event in the life of Lincoln. The five sculptured panels form the wall of the memorial court at the Memorial, and nine inscriptions selected from Lincoln's writings are engraved above the panels.

Kentucky 1809–1816 (the childhood years of Lincoln). This panel depicts Lincoln's life on the Sinking Spring and Knob Creek farms. On the far left is Jesse LaFollette, grandfather of Senator Robert LaFollette of Wisconsin and a Knob Creek neighbor of the Lincolns. Thomas Lincoln stands next to him, and Christopher Columbus Graham, who attended the wedding of Lincoln's parents, is seated. Lincoln, age seven, is listening to Graham's story, and Nancy Hanks Lincoln stands next to her son. His sister, Sarah, stands at the churn. One of Lincoln's schoolteachers, Caleb Hazel, is at the right.

11. *Indiana 1816–1830* (the boyhood days of Lincoln). Lincoln, a fully grown youth, stands holding an ax in the middle of the figures. At his far left is James Gentry, who sent his son, Allen, and Lincoln from Rockport, Indiana, to New Orleans with a flatboat loaded with salable items in 1828. Next to Gentry is Josiah Crawford, a neighbor from whom Lincoln borrowed books. Holding a hewn log are Aaron Grigsby, husband of Lincoln's sister, and Dennis F. Hanks, his mother's cousin and husband of his stepsister, Elizabeth Johnston. On the right are Allen Gentry, Lincoln's boat-mate on the trip to New Orleans, and Lincoln's stepmother, Sarah Bush Johnston Lincoln.

12. *Illinois 1830-1861* (the years of political ascendancy). Lincoln accepts congratulations from his friends on his election to the United States House of Representatives in 1846. Depicted left to right are his first and second law partners, John T. Stuart and Stephen T. Logan. Lincoln's special friend, Joshua Speed, with whom he first lived in Springfield, is shaking his hand. William H. "Billie" Herndon, his third and last law partner, stands between Lincoln and Speed. Simon Francis, publisher of the *Sangamon Journal,* is seated. Mary Todd Lincoln stands next to Francis and Orville H. Browning, friend and sometimes critic of Lincoln.

13. *Washington 1861–1865* (the years of command). President Abraham Lincoln visits General Ulysses S. Grant at Grant's headquarters in City Point, Virginia, March 25–April 3, 1865. The four soldiers represent the bravery and determination that made possible the victory at Appomattox Court House and the preservation of the Union.

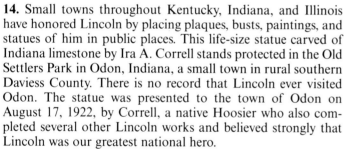

14. Small towns throughout Kentucky, Indiana, and Illinois have honored Lincoln by placing plaques, busts, paintings, and statues of him in public places. This life-size statue carved of Indiana limestone by Ira A. Correll stands protected in the Old Settlers Park in Odon, Indiana, a small town in rural southern Daviess County. There is no record that Lincoln ever visited Odon. The statue was presented to the town of Odon on August 17, 1922, by Correll, a native Hoosier who also completed several other Lincoln works and believed strongly that Lincoln was our greatest national hero.

15. This bronze statue of a seated Lincoln, sculptured by Henry Hering in 1934, is in University Park at the corner of New York and Pennsylvania streets in Indianapolis, Indiana. President Lincoln's stovepipe hat rests beneath the back of the chair. The statue was a gift of Henry C. Long, Civil War veteran and admirer of Lincoln, who left money in his will for this purpose.

Years in Illinois, to 1858
(Nos. 16–38)

16. A bronze statue depicts the twenty-one-year-old Lincoln walking at the side of the carved limestone bas-relief of the Thomas Lincoln family caravan entering the State of Illinois on March 6, 1830. It stands along a highway on the west bank of the Wabash River opposite Vincennes, Indiana. Both works were executed by Nellie V. Walker and presented to the State of Illinois on June 14, 1938. The spot marks the beginning of the Lincoln Heritage Trail in Illinois, established in 1963 to promote tourism in Kentucky, Indiana, and Illinois. The Lincoln emigrants included the Thomas Lincoln family (Thomas, Abraham, John D. Johnston, and Sarah Bush Johnston Lincoln); Mrs. Lincoln's two daughters, Elizabeth and Matilda, and their husbands, Dennis F. Hanks and Squire Levi Hall, and her five grandchildren, four Hanks and one Hall. The eldest of the grandchildren was eight years old, the youngest less than one year old.

The third-person autobiography Lincoln prepared for John L. Scripps in 1860 states:

> *March 1st 1830—A. having just completed his 21st year, his father and family, with the families of the two daughters and sons-in-law, of his step-mother, left the old homestead in Indiana, and came to Illinois. Their mode of conveyance was waggons drawn by ox-teams, or A. drove one of the teams. They reached the county of Macon, and stopped there some time within the same month of March. His father and family settled a new place on the North side of the Sangamon river, at the junction of*

> *the timber-land and prairie, about ten miles Westerly from Decatur. Here they built a log-cabin, into which they removed, and made sufficient of rails to fence ten acres of ground, fenced and broke the ground, and raised a crop of sow[n] corn upon it the same year. . . . During that winter [1831], A. together with his step-mother's son, John D. Johnston, and John Hanks, yet residing in Macon county, hired themselves to one Denton Offutt, to take a flat boat from Beardstown, Illinois to New Orleans; and for that purpose, were to join him—Offutt—at Springfield, Ills so soon as the snow should go off. When it did go off which was about the 1st. of March 1831—the county was so flooded, as to make traveling by land impracticable; to obviate which difficulty the[y] purchased a large canoe and came down the Sangamon river in it. This is the time and the manner of A's first entrance into Sangamon County. They found Offutt at Springfield, but learned from him that he failed in getting a boat at Beardstown. This led to their hiring themselves to him at $12 per month; each; and getting timber out of the trees and building a boat at old Sangamon Town on the Sangamon river, seven miles N.W. of Springfield, which boat they took to New Orleans, subsequently upon the old contract . . .*

> *During this boat enterprise acquaintance with Offutt, who was previously an entire stranger, he conceived a liking for A. and believing he could turn him to account, he contracted with him to act as clerk for*

him, on his return from New Orleans, in charge of a store and Mill at New-Salem, then in Sangamon, now in Menard county.

Lincoln returned from New Orleans to New Salem late in July 1831. This settlement of log cabin homes and businesses never had more than twenty-five families at its peak. It was a typical frontier village serving the surrounding community. Its founders expected economic and population growth, which never occurred. Before it became a deserted village in 1840, it boasted a cooper, cobbler, hatter, wheelwright, blacksmith, physician, tavern, post office, two stores, and two saloons. The village would be unknown today had Abraham Lincoln not made it his home for nearly six years.

In that frontier village Lincoln made friends and entered into such social and business life as the community offered. Using a book of legal forms he had purchased, he became a willing and gratuitous drafter of deeds, mortgages, and other legal forms for villagers who lacked such skills. He also served as a clerk in the Offutt store (which failed within a year), entered politics by announcing his candidacy for the lower

house of the state legislature, and joined the state militia for the Black Hawk War in April 1832. Returning from military service, he once more tried storekeeping in partnership with William F. Berry. That enterprise failed, as did his first bid for a seat in the legislature. In May 1833 he was appointed postmaster of New Salem by President Andrew Jackson and served in that role until May 1836. He served as the deputy surveyor of Sangamon County from 1834 to 1836.

Politics and law were the twin vocations that liberated Lincoln from the dying village of New Salem. He was elected to the lower house of the state legislature in 1834 and served three additional terms. During the campaign of 1834 he met John Todd Stuart, a fellow legislator from Springfield, who encouraged him to read and to study law. He borrowed books from Stuart, studied during his spare time, received his license to practice law on September 9, 1836, and was enrolled by a clerk of the state supreme court on March 1, 1837. He left New Salem for Springfield in April 1837, and Springfield was his home until he left for Washington on February 11, 1861, for his inauguration as the sixteenth president of the United States.

17. After traveling from Indiana in March 1830, the Lincoln family, with the aid of John Hanks, built this log cabin near the Sangamon River in Macon County in central Illinois and broke sod to raise a crop of corn. The next winter, the family endured the terrible cold and snow until March 1831, when, with the exception of Abraham and his stepbrother, John D. Johnston, they abandoned the cabin and moved to Coles County in eastern Illinois. Abraham and John took a flatboat down to New Orleans for Denton Offutt. After President Lincoln's death in 1865, the log cabin was dismantled, rebuilt, and displayed by Dennis and John Hanks on many occasions in cities in the United States. The original log cabin eventually was lost, and in 1975 it was replicated in Fairview Park in Decatur, the seat of Macon County. This replica was destroyed by an accidental fire in 1990.

[Photo copyrighted by the *Decatur Herald and Review*]

18. This bronze of Lincoln seated with an ax was executed by Fred M. Torrey, presented to the State of Illinois in 1946, and placed on West Main Street on the campus of James Millikin University in Decatur. The marble base has the inscription *"AT TWENTY-ONE I CAME TO ILLINOIS."*

The Lincoln emigrant caravan, of three wagons, two ox-driven and one horse-drawn, camped on the Decatur square on March 14, 1830. A small replica of this work is in the Lincoln Tomb in Springfield. Two other original statues by Torrey, *Lincoln the Ranger* and *Lincoln the Circuit Rider,* are also in the Tomb.

19. The city of Decatur further commemorated Lincoln by placing this bronze work by Antonio Vestuto on Lincoln Square on October 12, 1968. It symbolizes Lincoln's first political speech. A marker states that the young, barefoot "Lincoln mounted a stump by Harrell's Tavern facing the square and defended the Illinois Whig Party candidates near this spot at age 21 in the summer of 1830."

20. Anna Hyatt Huntington sculptured *Abraham Lincoln on the Prairie* and, along with Carleton Smith, president of the National Arts Foundation, presented it to the State of Illinois. This equestrian statue showing Lincoln reading a book stands along the highway south of Petersburg, Illinois, near the entrance to New Salem State Park. In 1906 William Randolph Hearst visited the ruins of New Salem, where Lincoln had lived from 1831 to 1837. The wealthy publisher was moved to purchase the site, and he gave it in trust to an old-settlers organization. In 1918 the Illinois legislature voted to take over the site, convert it into a state park, and restore the buildings. Restoration of New Salem Village began in 1932, and today the park is a major tourist attraction.

21. Abraham Lincoln, student and railsplitter, with a book in one hand and an ax in the other, greets tourists at the Visitor Center at New Salem State Park. The bronze statue, cast by Avard T. Fairbanks in 1953, stands on a marble base. It was "presented to the State of Illinois by the National Society of Utah Pioneers—1954, Nicholas C. Morgan, Sr., president and donor."

22. This bronze statue of Lincoln as a soldier commemorates his service in the Black Hawk War in spring and summer of 1832. Sculptured by Leonard Crunelle, it stands at Fort Dixon on the north shore of the Rock River between the Lincoln and Reagan bridges in Dixon, Illinois. While living in New Salem, Lincoln served eighty-one days as a captain and a private during this brief war, but saw no action. For his service he received $125 and a land grant in the Iowa Territory. Much later, in 1859, he viewed his election as captain of the volunteer militia company as "a success which gave me more pleasure than any I have had since." A small replica of this Crunelle work is in the Lincoln Tomb.

23. The restored Denton Offutt store stands in New Salem State Park. In spring 1831 Offutt had employed Lincoln and his stepbrother to take a flatboat of goods to New Orleans, and upon his return Lincoln clerked in the store from September 1831 until spring 1832, when the store failed and Offutt moved to Kentucky. For his first job that did not require hard physical labor, young Lincoln was paid fifteen dollars a month and had the privilege of sleeping in the store.

24. Lincoln became a storekeeper in 1832 after the Offutt store failed, and he and his partner, William Berry, owned two stores successively. The now-restored first Berry–Lincoln store was constructed at New Salem in 1831 by the Herndon brothers, James and Rowan. James sold his interest to Berry in 1832, and later that year Rowan sold his interest to Lincoln, for which Lincoln offered his promissory note. The store provided a good place for political discussions and storytelling, and Lincoln probably read law books in his spare time.

In August 1832 Lincoln ran for a seat in the Illinois House of Representatives. He lost, finishing eighth in a field of thirteen, but he received 277 of the 300 votes cast in the New Salem precinct.

25. The restored second Berry–Lincoln store building, constructed in 1831, was New Salem's sole frame structure. The partners purchased the store on January 15, 1833. In April Lincoln sold his interest to Berry. The store failed, and Berry died in 1835 with an estate of less than one hundred dollars. Lincoln became liable for partnership obligations amounting to about $1,100—a fortune for Lincoln. He spent several years paying off the debt.

On May 7, 1833, President Jackson appointed Lincoln to be New Salem's postmaster, a position that allowed him more time to read the law. On August 4, 1834, Lincoln was elected to the Ninth General Assembly of the State of Illinois. This time he ran second in a field of thirteen (five were elected). Later that year he took his seat as one of the fifty-five members of the House of Representatives at the capital in Vandalia.

26. This bronze statue of Lincoln carved by Albert L. Van den Bergen stands in Mr. Lincoln Square in Clinton, Illinois. It was dedicated on May 11, 1931. Inscribed on the base at the back of the statue are these words: "That it may not be forgotten that here for more than 9 years as a lawyer and friend he was counselor and teacher of our forefathers this statue is erected by the citizens of DeWitt County to the memory of Abraham Lincoln." From 1834 to 1857 DeWitt County was part of the Eighth Judicial Circuit and Clinton was the county seat where the court convened. Here in 1840 Lincoln and Stephen A. Douglas appeared as co-counsel in the county's first murder trial. And it was in a speech in Clinton in the summer of 1858 that Lincoln reportedly said: "You can fool all the people some of the time, and some of the people all the time, but you can not fool all the people all the time." These words are inscribed on the front of the base of the statue.

PUBLIC LANDS IN ILLINOIS.

JANUARY 17, 1839.

Read, laid on the table, and ordered to be printed.

Mr. LINCOLN, from the Committee on Finance, made the following

REPORT:

The Committee on Finance, to which was referred a resolution of this House instructing them to inquire into the expediency of proposing to purchase of the Government of the United States all the unsold lands lying within the limits of the State of Illinois, have had the same under consideration, and report:

That, in their opinion, if such purchase could be made on reasonable terms, two objects of high importance to the State might thereby be effected—first, acquire control over all the territory within the limits of the State—and, second, acquire an important source of revenue.

We will examine these two points in their order, and with special reference to their bearing upon our internal improvement system.

In the first place, then, we are now so far advanced in a general system of internal improvements that, if we would, we cannot retreat from it without disgrace and great loss. The conclusion then is, that we *must* advance; and, if so, the first reason for the State acquiring title to the public land is, that while we are at great expense in improving the country, and thereby enhancing the value of all the real property within its limits, that enhancement may attach exclusively to property owned by *ourselves* as a State, or to its citizens as individuals, and *not* to that owned by the Government of the United States. Again, it is conceded every where, as we believe, that Illinois surpasses every other spot of equal extent upon the face of the globe, in *fertility* of soil, and in the proportionable amount of the same which is sufficiently level for actual cultivation; and consequently that she is endowed by nature with the capacity of sustaining a greater amount of agricultural wealth and population than any other equal extent of territory in the world. To such an amount of wealth and population, our internal improvement system, now so alarming, in view of its having to be borne by our present numbers, and with our present means, would be a burden of no sort of consequence. How important, then, is it that all our energies should be exerted to bring that wealth and population among us as speedily as possible. But what, it may be asked, can the ownership of the land by the State do towards the accomplishment of that desirable object? It may be answered that the chief obstruction to the more rapid settlement of our country is found in

27. John Todd Stuart (1807–1895) was Lincoln's first law partner, from 1837 to 1841. Lincoln met Stuart in 1832 while both were serving in the Black Hawk War, Stuart as a major and Lincoln as a captain. It was Stuart who urged Lincoln to study law and loaned him books appropriate for self-study. Stuart was one of the early lawyers in Springfield, having been admitted to the bar in 1827.

Stuart and Lincoln served together in the Illinois General Assembly, and in 1838 Stuart defeated Stephen A. Douglas for a seat in the United State House of Representatives, where he served until 1843. From the beginning of the partnership, Lincoln managed most of the work of the firm, for Stuart spent much of his time on Whig politics and serving in the U.S. Congress. The firm of Stuart and Lincoln was the leading one in Springfield. During each of the four years of the partnership, Lincoln handled more than twenty-five cases in the spring and fall terms of the Sangamon Circuit Court. The cases covered the entire range of litigation, from small collection cases to homicide. The partnership was dissolved amicably in 1841.

Stuart, a cousin of Mary Todd Lincoln, later became a Democrat, Lincoln a Republican. Stuart was again elected to the U.S. House in 1862 and became a member opposed to Lincoln's policies. After Lincoln's death, Stuart oversaw the erection of the Lincoln Tomb as one of the directors of the National Lincoln Monument Association.

[Photograph courtesy of the Illinois State Historical Library]

28. This bill, the creative product of Lincoln's 1839 Committee on Finance in the Illinois legislature, was a scheme to finance the massive, financially troubled internal improvement program (railroads, turnpikes, bridges, rivers, and canals) voted by the Tenth Illinois General Assembly, 1836–1837. It proposed that the state purchase all the unsold land still part of the public domain within the state (an estimated twenty million acres) for twenty-five cents an acre. The state would then sell the lands to individuals at the Federal price of $1.25 an acre and thus have enough surplus to keep the program alive. The resolution passed the General Assembly, but the U.S. Congress took no action on the proposal.

29. The old Statehouse in Vandalia, Illinois, is shown as it appeared in 1994. Vandalia became the capital in 1820, replacing Kaskaskia. This building was constructed in 1836–1837 in a futile effort to forestall the movement of the capital from this town in south central Illinois. Lincoln received much of his early political training here while serving in the Tenth and Eleventh General Assemblies. On February 8, 1837, the General Assembly voted to move the capital to Springfield. Instrumental in forcing this move were the "Long Nine," the delegation from Sangamon County (Springfield was the county seat), all of whom were over six feet tall; Lincoln was one of their leaders. On January 4, 1839, Springfield became the new capital of Illinois. The Vandalia structure is now a State Historic Site managed by the Illinois Historic Preservation Agency.

30. Stephen Trigg Logan (1800–1880) was Lincoln's second law partner. Considered one of the finest lawyers in the state, he was an exacting partner, influential in stimulating Lincoln to become a better attorney. Lincoln and Logan met in 1832 while Lincoln was running for the legislature. Logan had left his native Kentucky earlier that year and was practicing law in Springfield. He was elected to the state legislature on several occasions.

Lincoln joined Logan's firm in 1841, and the offices were located on the third floor of the newly constructed Tinsley Building, across the street from the Illinois Statehouse. The partnership, one of the leading firms in the state, also was advantageously located near the State Supreme Court, the United States District Court, and the Sangamon Circuit Court. In addition to the usual range of litigation, the partnership found a profitable source of income in bankruptcy and divorce cases.

After Lincoln left the firm on friendly terms in 1844, Logan formed a partnership with his son, David. For more than two decades Logan and Lincoln remained close friends and political allies. In 1860 Logan served as a delegate to the Republican National Convention in Chicago, which nominated Lincoln for the presidency.

[Photograph courtesy of the Illinois State Historical Library]

31. William Henry "Billie" Herndon (1818–1891) was Lincoln's third and final law partner. Their partnership began in 1844 and lasted until Lincoln's death. Herndon is perhaps better known as Lincoln's biographer, the author of *Herndon's Lincoln: The True Story of a Great Life,* written in collaboration with Jesse W. Weik. The book, published several years after Lincoln's death, has been alternately criticized and praised. It contains much information on the pre-presidential years, including an exaggerated version of the Lincoln–Ann Rutledge romance. Highly questionable and unflattering pronouncements in the book concerning Mary Todd Lincoln cannot be verified.

Herndon became a clerk in the store of Joshua Speed in Springfield and started his acquaintance with Lincoln in 1837, when both roomed above Speed's store. Herndon was admitted to the bar on December 9, 1844, and the two formed the firm of Lincoln and Herndon that year, taking over the space in the Tinsley Building that had been occupied by Logan and Lincoln. Lincoln did most of the courtroom work, while Herndon managed the office and did searches for precedents. By the 1850s the partners were lawyers for approximately twenty percent of the cases tried in the Sangamon Circuit Court and their firm had an active appellate practice in the Illinois Supreme Court.

In 1854 Herndon became mayor of Springfield, which had slightly more than 6,000 inhabitants. An active, reform mayor, the hard-drinking Herndon became a strong advocate of prohibition. No one urged him to seek reelection after his term expired in 1855, but he served several years as one of the three bank commissioners for the State of Illinois. Both before and after Lincoln's death, Herndon gave lectures on temperance but frequently "fell off the wagon." Just before leaving Springfield for Washington to assume the presidency, Lincoln bluntly questioned Herndon about his drinking habits.

Lincoln's law career is linked inseparably to itinerant practice on the Eighth Judicial Circuit, where he did much of his legal work. In spring and fall, state supreme justices and later elected circuit judges traveled the circuit hearing civil and criminal cases in many county seats. Lawyers followed the judges and were usually assisted by local lawyers, who did the preliminary work before the case came to court. From 1839 until 1860 (except in 1847–1849, when he served in the U.S. House of Representatives) Lincoln rode the large Eighth Judicial Circuit. He found it rewarding, for there he formed lasting friendships with lawyers and judges who were instrumental in winning his nomination for the presidency in 1860. On the negative side, riding the circuit meant that for several months of the year he was away from the family he dearly loved. Court days were big days on the Illinois prairie, and people flocked into the county seat to look, listen, trade, and visit.

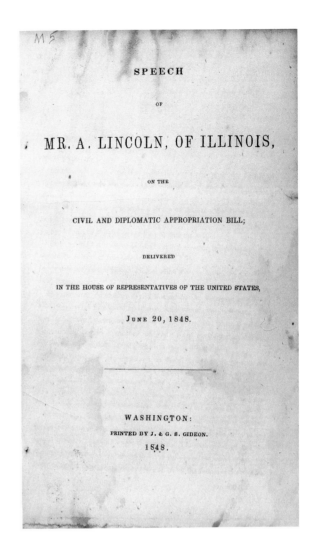

SPEECH

OF

MR. A. LINCOLN, OF ILLINOIS,

ON THE

CIVIL AND DIPLOMATIC APPROPRIATION BILL;

DELIVERED

IN THE HOUSE OF REPRESENTATIVES OF THE UNITED STATES,

JUNE 20, 1848.

WASHINGTON:

PRINTED BY J. & G. S. GIDEON.

1848.

32. The earliest known photograph of Abraham Lincoln, this daguerreotype was made in 1846 by N. H. Shepherd, who had a studio in Springfield. It is thought that the photograph was taken shortly after the thirty-seven-year-old Lincoln had been elected (on August 3) to the Thirteenth United States Congress (1847–1849). Eleven years elapsed before Lincoln posed for another photograph.

33. U.S. Representative Lincoln pointed out the logic of internal improvements at Federal expense in this House speech, a reply to a veto of a river and harbor bill by President Polk. Lincoln, representing the Seventh Congressional District, was the lone Whig congressman from Illinois. His congressional career was not distinguished. He opposed the war against Mexico, declaring it a war of aggression. Since the war was popular in Illinois, he was condemned by the Democratic party press as a modern Benedict Arnold.

Lincoln did not seek a second term. By agreement with two other prominent Illinois Whigs, each would rotate for election to the office. He had given his word, and he kept it.

34. The law firm of Lincoln and Herndon occupied the north portion of the third floor of the Tinsley Building at the corner of Adams and Sixth streets in Springfield from 1844 to 1847. When Lincoln served in the Congress, starting in 1847, Herndon moved to a smaller space at the south end of the third floor. The building, constructed in 1840, has undergone extensive renovation, as this 1994 photograph reveals. In 1847 the firm moved its offices to a building on South Fifth Street that was later demolished.

35. This second known photograph of Lincoln was taken by Alexander Hesler in Chicago in February 1857. Lincoln referred to it in a letter he wrote to James F. Babcock on September 13, 1860: "The original of the picture you inclose, and which I return, was taken from life, and is, I think a very true one; though my wife, and many others, do not. My impression is that their objection arises from the disordered condition of the hair. My judgement is worth nothing in these matters."

36. *Lincoln the Lawyer* by Lorado Zadoc Taft is a bronze statue that stands in Carle Park, across the street from Urbana High School in Urbana, Illinois. Taft was born in Elmwood, Illinois, in 1860 and earned two degrees from the University of Illinois in Urbana. From Urbana he went to Paris, where he studied at the Ecole des Beaux-Arts for three years. He taught for many years at the Art Institute of Chicago, lectured widely, and wrote many publications relating to the arts. Lincoln visited Urbana, the county seat of Champaign County, twice yearly, for it was in the Eighth Judicial Circuit. He tried his first case for the Illinois Central Railroad there in May 1853: *McGinnis v. Illinois Central Railroad.*

This statue, unveiled on July 3, 1937, was made possible through a legacy in the will of Judge and Mrs. J. O. Cunningham. Judge Cunningham was a friend of Lincoln and later of Lorado Taft and his family. Inscribed on its base are portions of a speech Lincoln gave in Peoria, Illinois, on October 16, 1854, and one he delivered on December 31, 1862. A small replica of this work is in the Lincoln Tomb.

37. This bronze statue of a young Lincoln seated reading a book was sculptured by Robert Merrill Gage and dedicated on May 27, 1961. It is on the campus of Lincoln College in Lincoln, Illinois, the only town said to be named for him while he was still alive. Lincoln was invited to the new unnamed town in Logan County to help sell lots, record their sale, and write a town charter. Someone suggested naming the town Lincoln, and Abraham himself is said to have christened it with watermelon juice on August 27, 1853. Lincoln frequently visited Logan County, part of the Eighth Judicial Circuit.

On November 21, 1860, President-elect Lincoln spoke here on his way to Chicago, and his funeral train made its last stop in Lincoln on May 3, 1865, before reaching its final destination, Springfield.

38. Amon T. Joslin made this ambrotype in Danville, Illinois, in May 1857, at the request of Thomas J. Hilyard, deputy sheriff of Vermilion County. Lincoln was in Danville acting for the defendant in a case, *Leverick v. Leverick,* at the Vermilion Circuit Court. The jury found the defendant insane.

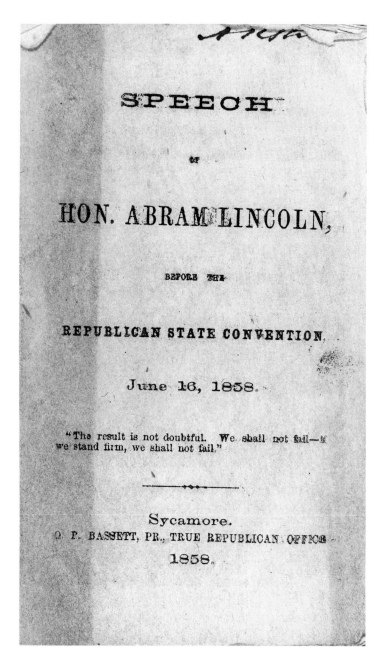

SPEECH

of

HON. ABRAM LINCOLN,

BEFORE THE

REPUBLICAN STATE CONVENTION.

June 16, 1858.

"The result is not doubtful. We shall not fail—if we stand firm, we shall not fail."

Sycamore.
O. P. BASSETT, PR., TRUE REPUBLICAN OFFICE.
1858.

Campaign for the U.S. Senate
(Nos. 39–55)

39. This report of the proceedings of the second Republican State Convention held in Illinois in 1858 contains Lincoln's "House Divided" speech, which he made in accepting the Republican nomination for the U.S. Senate against the incumbent Democrat, Stephen A. Douglas:

> *A house divided against itself cannot stand. I believe this government cannot endure permanently, half slave and half free. I do not expect the Union to be dissolved—I do not expect the house to fall—but I do expect it will cease to be divided. It will become all one thing, or all the other.*

This speech was considered by many to be a radical antislavery declaration. It was certainly the most radical antislavery address Lincoln ever made, aimed primarily at Douglas, who favored "popular sovereignty" in maintaining that territorial residents could permit or exclude slavery within their domain at the ballot box.

At the first Republican State Convention, held in Bloomington, Illinois, in 1856, Lincoln had given a rousing concluding address, now called the "Lost Speech" because it was never recorded. During the 1856 presidential campaign, Lincoln spoke frequently throughout Illinois on behalf of John C. Frémont, the first Republican party nominee for president of the United States.

POLITICAL DEBATES

BETWEEN

HON. ABRAHAM LINCOLN

AND

HON. STEPHEN A. DOUGLAS,

In the Celebrated Campaign of 1858, in Illinois;

INCLUDING THE PRECEDING SPEECHES OF EACH, AT CHI-
CAGO, SPRINGFIELD, ETC.; ALSO, THE TWO GREAT
SPEECHES OF MR. LINCOLN IN OHIO, IN 1859,

AS

CAREFULLY PREPARED BY THE REPORTERS OF EACH PARTY, AND PUBLISHED
AT THE TIMES OF THEIR DELIVERY.

———————

COLUMBUS:
FOLLETT, FOSTER AND COMPANY.
BOSTON: BROWN & TAGGARD. NEW YORK: W. A. TOWNSEND & CO.
CHICAGO: S. C. GRIGGS & CO. DETROIT: PUTNAM, SMITH & CO.
1860.

---

40. The debates between Lincoln, the Republican challenger, and two-term Democratic incumbent Stephen A. Douglas, candidates from Illinois for a seat in the U.S. Senate in 1858, are perhaps the best known and still the greatest forensic performances in American history. The two men faced off in seven formal debates held in seven of the nine Illinois congressional districts. (Springfield and Chicago were not included; both Lincoln and Douglas had already given speeches there.) The debates were held in Ottawa, Freeport, Jonesboro, Charleston, Galesburg, Quincy, and Alton, in that order.

The two political opponents agreed to alternate openings and closings of the speechmaking on the same platform. One hour was given to the opening statement, one and one-half hours to a response, and one-half hour for rebuttal. The slavery issue, an ongoing topic that dominated political thinking nationally, consumed the debates, which were attended by all of the pageantry the two political parties could muster, including pre- and post-debate parties; parades of men, women, children, and horses; banners, signs, honor guards, and bands of musicians. Douglas even brought his own cannon, which fired a salute in his honor upon his arrival at each debate site. Reporters representing the press of both political parties recorded every spoken word and estimated the size of the crowds, which were large by 1858 standards. The greatest atten-

dance, some 15,000, was at the Galesburg debate; the least, 1,500, was at tiny Jonesboro in southern Illinois.

Even though Lincoln gained the majority of the popular vote—125,430 votes to Douglas's 121,609—the outdated apportionment law insured Douglas's reelection by the Illinois legislature, 54 to 46. But Lincoln was the eventual winner: he gained national recognition as a result of his newspaper exposure, later received the Republican nomination for the presidency, and was elected President of the United States in 1860.

The debates were first published in book form as a presidential campaign document in 1860. The idea for it is attributed to Lincoln, who gathered newspaper clippings of the speeches during the debates and placed them in a scrapbook that was made available to Follet and Foster of Columbus, Ohio, the firm that published them. Lincoln received one hundred copies for distribution to friends and he autographed many of them. The copy in The Lilly Library is inscribed in pencil to: "Stephen S. Winchester, Esq. With compliments of A. Lincoln."

In August, September, and October of 1994 each debate was reenacted in the debate cities by local clubs and civic groups. Personnel in period costumes, military bands, parties, and festivals were present at each debate. The reenactments were simulated and telecast nationally by the cable network, C-SPAN.

41. Freeport, in northwestern Illinois, hosted the second Lincoln–Douglas debate on a cool, damp August 27, 1858. The debate site, in downtown Freeport near North State Avenue and East Douglas Street, is now referred to as Debate Square. A boulder with a plaque commemorating the event was placed in the square in 1902, and on January 3, 1903, President Theodore Roosevelt dedicated it. Also on the square is this bronze work, *Lincoln and Douglas in Debate,* with its life-size figures of Lincoln and Douglas. Lincoln is seated with his hat beside him on the platform; Douglas is standing and speaking. This work by Lily Tolpo of Stockton, Illinois, was dedicated on August 27, 1992. Copies of the work were to be made available for placement at the six other debate sites.

42. Individual plaques of Lincoln and Douglas commemorate their fifth debate, held on the campus of Knox College in Galesburg on a cold and windy October 7, 1858. Cast by Avard Tennyson Fairbanks, the plaques grace the east entrance to Old Main, outside of which the debate took place. Of all the buildings that were debate sites, Old Main at Knox College is the only one that still stands and is in use today. In spite of the inclement weather, a crowd estimated at over 15,000 attended, the largest group to attend any of the seven debates.

In this debate Lincoln asserted that the Declaration of Independence encompassed negroes—a radical statement at that time. He contended that slaves were "created equal" and endowed with "certain unalienable rights" such as "life, liberty and the pursuit of happiness." He had a friendly audience for this thesis, for Knox County and its surrounding counties were strongly antislavery.

43. This large bronze statue, *Lincoln the Debater,* stands in Taylor's Park on the northeast side of Freeport. Executed by Leonard Crunelle and presented to the City of Freeport by the Honorable T. W. Rawleich, it was dedicated on the seventy-first anniversary of the debate in 1929. A small replica of this work is in the Lincoln Tomb.

44. This large bronze relief, set in limestone in Washington Park in downtown Quincy, commemorates the sixth of the Lincoln–Douglas debates, held on a cloudy October 13, 1858. Lorado Taft completed this memorial shortly before his death on October 30, 1936, and it was dedicated on December 18, 1936. Quotations from the speeches of both debaters, selected by Lincoln historian Paul Angle, are engraved on the back of the memorial. The original plaster cast of this work has been restored and put on display in the atrium of the College of Law building of the University of Illinois in Champaign.

45. In addition to the seven formal debates, both Lincoln and Douglas spoke frequently throughout Illinois in 1858. Lincoln made more than fifty campaign speeches statewide. He also sat for at least ten photographs, many taken at the request of friends who found his likeness a desirable possession as his reputation grew. This photo, a glass ambrotype, was taken by Samuel G. Alschuler at Urbana on April 25, 1858. The velvet-collared jacket Lincoln is wearing was lent to him by the photographer, who thought the candidate's old linen duster would not photograph well. Not revealed in the photograph is one untoward result: the sleeves were too short for Lincoln's long arms.

46. In this ambrotype taken by Abraham Byers at Beardstown, Illinois, on May 7, 1858, Lincoln is wearing his white linen suit. He had been in the Cass County courtroom that day successfully and gratuitously defending Duff Armstrong, the son of a New Salem friend, against a murder charge. Using an almanac, Lincoln discredited the state's main witness by showing that there was insufficient moonlight on the night of the murder for the witness to see what he had described in detail. The old Cass County Courthouse where the trial took place still stands and is used as the Beardstown City Hall. The county seat of Cass County was subsequently moved from Beardstown to the nearby town of Virginia.

47. This ambrotype was taken by Preston Butler in Springfield, Illinois—probably in July 1858—at the request of a friend of Lincoln's, Sylvester Strong of Atlanta, Illinois.

48. In the 1963 edition of Hamilton and Ostendorf, *Lincoln in Photographs*, the authors date this photograph by Polycarp Von Schneidau, Chicago, July 11, 1858. In the 1985 edition of their book, it is dated October 27, 1854.

49. This photograph of Lincoln was taken in Springfield, Illinois, in September 1858, at the request of Harriet Hanks Chapman, who had lived with the Lincolns in Springfield. She was the daughter of Elizabeth Johnston and Dennis F. Hanks and the granddaughter of Lincoln's stepmother, Sarah Bush Johnston Lincoln.

50. Lincoln campaigned in Pittsfield, a small town in western Illinois, and spoke there in the square for two hours on the afternoon of October 1, 1858. This ambrotype was taken in Pittsfield that day by Calvin Jackson at the request of D. H. Gilmer.

51. William Judkins Thomson took this ambrotype of Lincoln in Monmouth, in western Illinois, on October 11, 1858. Before his three-hour speech Lincoln was serenaded by the Monmouth Republican Glee Club. His talk was well received by a large crowd.

52. This ambrotype probably dates from late 1858. The photographer and place where it was taken are not definitely known. The Illinois towns of Monmouth, Peoria, Pittsfield, and Springfield; Dayton, Ohio; and Hannibal, Missouri, have been conjectured. It was reproduced on many campaign ribbons in 1860.

53. When and where Lincoln posed for this tintype are not known; neither is the photographer.

54. Samuel M. Fassett took this photograph of Lincoln at the gallery of Cooke and Fassett in Chicago on October 4, 1859.

55. The date, place, and photographer of this Lincoln photograph are unknown, though there are many conjectures.

First Presidential Campaign
(Nos. 56–104)

56. In the Wigwam, this temporary two-story wooden structure at Market and State streets in Chicago, delegates to the Second National Convention of the Republican party nominated Abraham Lincoln for president on the third ballot, May 18, 1860. Lincoln, who did not attend the convention, received the news of his nomination before noon in Springfield. On the following day he received formal notification, and on May 23, 1860, he formally accepted the nomination.

Lincoln had received a large measure of national recognition as a result of the Lincoln–Douglas debates in 1858 and his Cooper Institute speech in New York on February 27, 1860, which was followed by several appearances and speeches in Rhode Island, New Hampshire, and Connecticut. Still he was by no means as well known as the leading contender for the Republican nomination, William H. Seward, or the lesser ones, Salmon P. Chase and Simon Cameron. But he was more electable, as his friends and managers at the convention—David Davis, Leonard Swett, Norman B. Judd, Stephen T. Logan, Jesse Fell, Jesse Dubois, and Ward Hill Lamon among others—were quick to inform the delegates.

61. Mrs. Stephen A. Douglas, the former Adele Cutts, was Douglas's second wife. They were married in Washington in November 1856. A grandniece of Dolly Madison, she became a hostess of great charm. The splendid Douglas home was the setting for many grand social events.

62. Stephen Arnold Douglas (1813–1861) of Illinois, the Democratic candidate for president in 1860, was born in Vermont, moved to New York, and then settled in Illinois at Jacksonville. His small stature (five feet four inches) and his importance in Democratic politics earned him the title "Little Giant." He was nominated by a fragmented Democratic party; its southern branch nominated John C. Breckinridge. In the belief that the party split threatened to sever the Union, Douglas broke historical precedent, which had kept presidential candidates from actively campaigning, and stumped the United States both North and South. In the North he hoped to take votes from Lincoln; in the South he hoped to persuade southern Democrats to return to the party. He failed in both efforts. He finished second in the popular vote with 27 percent of the votes cast. In the Electoral College he won only Missouri's nine votes and three of New Jersey's seven.

After formation of the Confederate States of America, Douglas pledged his full support to Lincoln and urged all citizens to put aside partisan politics and support the Union. Senator Douglas died in Chicago at age forty-eight on June 3, 1861, after some weeks of illness. On the day of Douglas's funeral, June 7, President Lincoln closed all government departments to commemorate his distinguished political career.

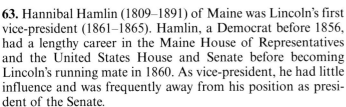

63. Hannibal Hamlin (1809–1891) of Maine was Lincoln's first vice-president (1861–1865). Hamlin, a Democrat before 1856, had a lengthy career in the Maine House of Representatives and the United States House and Senate before becoming Lincoln's running mate in 1860. As vice-president, he had little influence and was frequently away from his position as president of the Senate.

64. John Bell of Tennessee was the Constitutional Union party candidate for president in 1860. His running mate was the highly respected Edward Everett of Massachusetts. The party was composed of former Whig and American party members and others who found it impossible to join the Republican or the splintered Democratic party. Bell's party tried to maintain a moderate course between the radical antislavery Republicans and the fire-eating, proslavery southern Democrats. Its main support came from the border slave states. The Bell–Everett slate received a little more than 12 percent of the popular vote and thirty-nine Electoral College votes. It received a majority in Kentucky, Tennessee, and Virginia, but no votes at all in New Jersey, New York, and Rhode Island.

65. John C. Breckinridge of Kentucky was the 1860 presidential candidate of the anti-Douglas northern Democrats and the southern Democrats. Joseph Lane, a U.S. senator from Oregon, was his running mate. The southern Democrats, who had bolted from the Democratic Convention at Charleston, put forward a platform supporting slavery in the territories, admission of new states into the Union on an equal footing, and acquisition of Cuba. The Breckinridge–Lane ticket received 18 percent of the total popular vote and seventy-two electoral votes. It had a majority in Alabama, Arkansas, Delaware, Florida, Georgia, Maryland, Mississippi, North Carolina, South Carolina, and Texas, but received no votes in New Jersey, New York, and Rhode Island.

66. "The 'Wigwam' Grand March," written for the Republican presidential campaign of 1860, took its name from the temporary building constructed for the Republican National Convention in Chicago. Lincoln in life and in death generated more musical compositions than any other national figure, most of them published from 1860 through 1865—polkas, schottisches, quicksteps, marches, requiems. It will be noted that the portrait on the cover of the sheet music is of a beardless Lincoln. He did not start growing his beard until a few days after the election on November 6.

67. The Republican party kept printmakers, photographers, and portrait artists busy during the race for the White House in 1860. Party patrons flooded the northern states with copies of oil portraits of the candidates and lithographic prints copied from old and new photographs. The cartoon industry, an integral part of the lithographic business, was also active. Cartoons, sometimes gentle, sometimes critical, and infrequently savage, were common during the great propaganda blitz that preceded the election.

This hand-colored Currier & Ives lithograph of Lincoln and his running mate is titled *The Republican Banner for 1860.* Currier & Ives eventually published more than seventy-five lithographs of Lincoln, including his signing of the Emancipation Proclamation, his assassination, and his funeral. The firm also issued a number of political cartoons during the Lincoln Administration, many of them drawn by Louis Maurer and Ben Day.

68. This hand-colored Currier & Ives lithograph of Lincoln, circulated during the campaign of 1860, is based on a Mathew Brady photograph taken at the time of Lincoln's Cooper Institute speech. The facsimile signature increased its desirability.

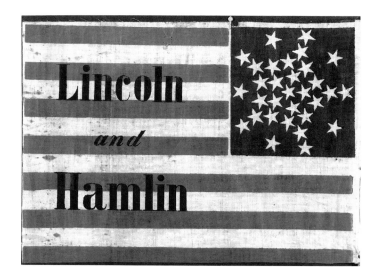

69. The Republicans used the American flag as a partisan banner in the campaign of 1860.

THE GREAT EXHIBITION OF 1860.

70. This hand-colored lithograph published by Currier & Ives exhibits several aspects of the 1860 election. Horace Greeley of the *New York Tribune,* who served as a delegate from Oregon at the Republican Convention, grinds away on his hand organ. Lincoln, who did not speak publicly on any issue after his nomination, has his mouth locked as he rides a rail labeled "Republican Platform." William H. Seward, a front-runner for the Republican nomination in 1860, holds a black child and implies that he is still the head Republican. Henry J. Raymond of the *New York Times* indicates that he has "my own little axe to grind," while James Watson Webb, publisher of the *Morning Courier* and the *New York Enquirer*, passes the tambourine asking for help.

71. This house at the corner of Eighth and Jackson streets in Springfield, the only home the Lincolns ever owned, was photographed in the summer of 1860 by John Adams Whipple of Boston. Presidential candidate Lincoln and son Willie (William Wallace) pose on the terrace, while the youngest Lincoln son, the seven-year-old Tad (Thomas) peeks out from behind the corner post. The two figures in the foreground are unidentified.

The house, a one-and-a-half-story cottage constructed in 1839, was purchased on January 16, 1844, from the Reverend Charles Dresser for $1,200 along with a town lot valued at $300. A second story added to the structure in 1856 cost $1,300. Before leaving Springfield to assume the presidency, Lincoln rented the house for $350 per year to Lucius Tilton, president of the Great Western Railroad. Reverend Dresser had married Abraham and Mary Lincoln at the home of Mary's older sister, Elizabeth (Mrs. Ninian Edwards), on November 4, 1842.

Paris Illinois June 1860
For the purpose of promoting the Republican
Cause and aiding in the Election of the republican
ticket, State as well as National the undersigned
form themselves into an organization to be known
as the Republican Wide Awakes of Paris,
1st
That the wide awakes being vindicators of Rep
ublican principles and seeking to enhance the suc
cess of the same, extend a cordial invitation to all
young men who are willing to endorse the sentiments
of the Republican party and will pledge themselves to
abide by the rules & regulations of the association.
2nd That every person becoming a member of
this association shall provide himself with a uni
form consisting of Cap, Cloak and Torch or shall
pay into the Treasury the sum of
which shall entitle him to those Equipments.
3rd That each member shall hold himself in read
iness to take part in Torch light processions

72. By 1994, when this photograph was taken, the Lincoln home had become a major tourist attraction. Following President Lincoln's assassination in April 1865, the house continued to be rented. Mary Lincoln died in 1882, and in 1887 Robert Todd Lincoln, her only surviving son, deeded the property to the State of Illinois. The state operated it until 1972, when it became the Lincoln Home National Historic Site, administered by the U.S. National Park Service. The Park Service also purchased and restored the four-square-block area around the Lincoln house and built a large visitors' center and parking lot.

73. The Wide Awakes were an important component of the Republican strategy in the presidential election of 1860. Organized throughout the North, they paraded in glazed capes and caps, carrying flaming torches, flags, and banners.

This is the secretary's book of the Republican Wide Awakes in Paris, Edgar County, Illinois. If the Paris Wide Awakes can be accepted as a prototype, the groups supported both the state and national Republican tickets. The appeal was "to all young men who are willing to endorse the sentiments of the Republican party." Each member was to "provide himself with a uniform consisting of Cap, Cloak, and Torch" and "shall hold himself in readiness to take part in Torch light processions during the Presidential Campaign, to perform escort duty to attend the night meetings and grand rallies of the party and to act as a vigilance committee on Election day." He was to "refrain from using profane language" on public occasions and "Comport himself in a decent and respectful manner." The Paris Wide Awakes enrolled 163 members and were active from June 6 until the November election. Weekly meetings featured singing and speeches, and members paraded in nearby towns in eastern Illinois on invitation. They also paraded in Terre Haute, Indiana, and had a large delegation at a mass meeting in Indianapolis.

74. Many specially printed envelopes circulated during the election campaign of 1860, including these two examples.

75. Horace Greeley, editor of the *New York Tribune* and an unsolicited adviser to Lincoln on many occasions, complained about presidential nominee Lincoln's lack of name recognition and offered a cure: "There should be at least one million copies of some cheap *Life of Lincoln.* There are thousands who do not yet know Abraham Lincoln."

This booklet is thought to be the first such life story published for the 1860 election. The publisher announced that the booklet was in press on the day after Lincoln was nominated, May 19. On June 2, it was advertised as "now ready." Written by an unknown author who did not know Lincoln's correct given name, this "Wigwam Edition" reportedly sold 12,000 copies within a week of publication. Though valueless as a life story, it is an important example of campaign literature of the day.

Twenty-one publications on the life of Lincoln have been recorded as printed during the 1860 campaign, some in more than one edition. The sale of these short biographies was brisk, but did not reach the magnitude desired by Greeley. One estimate is that no more than two or three hundred thousand copies of the "Wigwam Edition" were sold.

LIFE
OF
ABRAHAM LINCOLN.

CHAPTER I.

EARLY LIFE.

His Ancestors—His Grandfather Murdered by Indians—His Parents—An Only Child—Adverse Circumstances—Western Schools Fifty Years Ago—Removal to Indiana—Work in the Forest—Letter-Writer for the Neighborhood—The First Great Sorrow—Character of his Mother—Reading the Scriptures—Self-Educated—First Books—Interesting Incident of Boyhood—Early Western Preachers.

IT is not known at what period the ancestors of Abraham Lincoln came to America. The first account that has been obtained of them dates back about one hundred and fifty years, at which time they were living in Berks County, Pennsylvania, and were members of the Society of Friends. Whence or when they came to that region is not known.

About the middle of the last century, the great-grandfather of Abraham Lincoln removed from Berks County, Pennsylvania, to Rockingham County, Virginia. There Abraham Lincoln, the grandfather, and Thomas Lincoln, the father of the subject of this sketch, were born. Abraham, the grandfather, had four brothers—Isaac, Jacob, John, and Thomas—descendants of whom are now living in Virginia, North Carolina, Kentucky, Tennessee, and Missouri. Abraham removed to Kentucky about the year 1780, and four years thereafter, while engaged in opening a farm, he was surprised and killed by Indians; leaving a widow, three sons, and two daughters. The eldest son, Mordecai, remained in Kentucky until late in life, when he removed to Hancock County, Illinois, where he shortly afterward died, and where his descendants still live. The second son, Josiah, settled many years ago on Blue River, in Harrison County, Indiana. The eldest daughter, Mary, was married to Ralph Crume, and some of her descendants are now living in Breckenridge County, Kentucky. The second daughter, Nancy, was married to William Brumfield, and her descendants are supposed to be living in Kentucky.

Thomas, the youngest son, and father of the subject of this sketch, by the death of his father and the very narrow circumstances of his mother, was thrown upon his own resources while yet a child. Traveling from neighborhood to neighborhood, working wherever he could find employment, he grew up literally without education. He finally settled in Hardin County, where, in 1806, he was married to Nancy Hanks, whose family had also come from Virginia. The fruits of this union were a daughter and two sons. One of the latter died in infancy; the daughter died later in life, having been married, but leaving no issue. The sole survivor is the subject of this sketch.

Abraham Lincoln was born in Hardin County, Kentucky, February 12th, 1809. It would be difficult to conceive of more unpromising circumstances than those under which he was ushered into life. His parents were poor and uneducated. They were under the social ban which the presence of slavery always entails upon poverty. Their very limited means and the low grade of the neighboring schools, precluded the expectation of conferring upon their children the advantages of even a common English education. The present inhabitants of the Western States can have but a faint idea of the schools which fifty years ago constituted the only means of education accessible to the poorer classes. The teachers were, for the most part, ignorant, uncultivated men, rough of speech, uncouth in manners, and rarely competent to teach beyond the simplest rudiments of learning—"spelling, reading, writing," and sometimes a very little arithmetic. The books of study then in vogue, would not now be tolerated in schools of the lowest grade. The school-house, constructed of logs, floorless, windowless, and without inclosure, was in admirable harmony with teacher, text-books, and the mode of imparting instruction.

In his seventh year, Abraham was sent for short periods to two of these schools, and while attending them progressed so far as to learn to write. For this acquirement he manifested a great fondness. It was his custom to form letters, to write words and sen-

Das Leben
—von—
Abraham Lincoln

nebst einer kurzen Skizze des Lebens von
Hannibal Hamlin.

Chicago, 1860,
Druck der „Illinois Staats-Zeitung."

76. This campaign biography, *Life of Abraham Lincoln* by John Locke Scripps, was based on an interview with Lincoln and an autobiographical sketch (written in the third person) which Lincoln supplied in June 1860. The thirty-two-page booklet probably was published in mid-July. Its advertised price per 100 was $2.50; per 1,000, $20.00. Stephen B. Oates in *With Malice Toward None: The Life of Abraham Lincoln* reported that the Scripps biography sold more than one million copies.

77. This German-language edition of a life of Lincoln and a sketch of his running mate, Hannibal Hamlin, circulated during the 1860 presidential campaign.

78. For fifty cents, subscribers received thirteen numbers of the weekly *The Rail Splitter* during the presidential campaign of 1860. This is the first number, published on August 1. The editors, two Cincinnati physicians, J. H. Jordan and J. B. McKeehan, stated that 30,000 copies of this number were printed; in the second number, they stated that 15,000 copies were still available. This number and several others contained illustrations signed by Thee Jones. A similar Republican paper with the same name was published in Chicago from June 23 to October 27, eighteen numbers in all.

Lincoln was dubbed the "Rail Splitter" at the Illinois Republican Convention in Decatur on May 10, 1860, when the convention endorsed him for the presidency. The idea came from Richard J. Oglesby, a friend of Lincoln and future governor of Illinois. With John Hanks, a cousin of Nancy Hanks Lincoln, Oglesby went to rural Macon County and procured two rails thought to have been split by Lincoln shortly after he moved to Illinois in 1830. The two time-stained rails were paraded into the convention hall, the Wigwam, in Decatur, with a banner reading "Abraham Lincoln the Rail Candidate for President in 1860. Two rails from a lot of 3,000 made in 1830 by Thos. Hanks [should have read John Hanks] and Abe Lincoln—Whose Father was the First Pioneer of Macon County." Rails symbolizing Lincoln's humble origins became design elements on Lincoln's campaign literature.

79. "Honest Old Abe" was a campaign song in 1860. This sheet music's front cover features a facsimile signature of Lincoln and a hand-colored portrait based on an 1857 photograph by Alexander Hesler of Chicago.

The song's first verse mentions Lincoln's opponent Douglas by name.

> *Ye Democrats list to my story,*
> *Ye Douglasites all give me heed;*
> *Though your candidate's running for glory,*
> *He's not making very good speed.*

The other verses name the states represented by his two other opponents, Bell and Breckinridge.

Biographers of Lincoln emphasized his honesty in returning borrowed books, paying debts, and keeping political promises, and the "honest" sobriquet, used widely in the presidential campaign of 1860, was valuable in establishing Lincoln as a candidate the common person could trust. Although the press often referred to Lincoln as "Abe," friends and acquaintances never called him that after he reached maturity—it was always "Lincoln" or "Mr. Lincoln." Abe, the name his stepmother used, put the candidate on a level appreciated by voters.

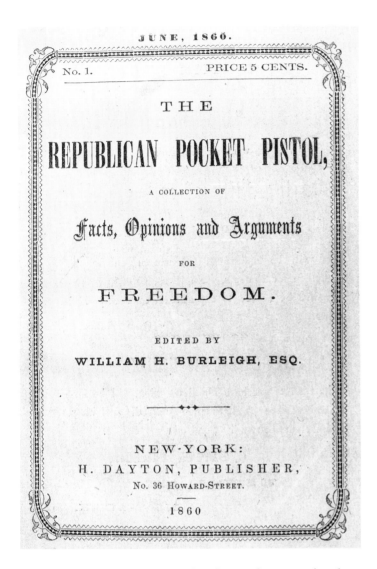

80. *The Republican Pocket Pistol*, an interesting campaign document with an intriguing name, circulated during the 1860 presidential campaign. Its publisher promised in the first number, shown here, that it would be published monthly "till the Presidential Election," stating that "its object is to present, in the most concise form practicable, the principles and aims of the Republican Party, the issues involved in its contest with the slave power and its Democratic allies." The price of each number was five cents but Republican clubs could purchase it for four dollars per hundred or thirty dollars per thousand. The editor, William Henry Burleigh, was a journalist and reformer who began lecturing for the American Anti-Slavery Society as early as 1836, and wrote and lectured for the New York Temperance Society. The Lilly Library has three numbers of this publication, dated June, July, and August 1860. Each number contains thirty-six pages.

81. The sheet music of this "Lincoln Quick Step" features a hand-colored, lithographed cover by artist Thomas Sinclair. The song was entered for copyright in 1860 by Lee & Walker of Philadelphia; the secondary publisher was H. M. Higgins of Chicago. The portrait of Lincoln was based on a Samuel M. Fassett photograph of 1859. The artwork on the cover depicts Lincoln as a rail splitter and as a flatboatman. The primary tools of the rail splitter (ax, wedge, and maul) are to the left of the portrait; those of the flatboatman (anchor, rudder, sweep-oar, and pole) are on the right. The only words to this quick step are these:

> *Honest Old Abe has split many rail*
> *He is up to his work, and he'll surely not fail,*
> *He has guided his Flat-Boat thro' many a strait*
> *And watchful he'll prove at the Helm of the State.*

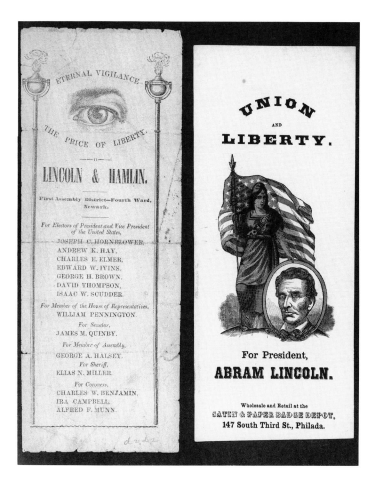

83. In campaign material for the 1860 election, the First Assembly District—Fourth Ward in Newark, New Jersey, shows its support for the Lincoln–Hamlin ticket (left), while the Satin & Paper Badge Depot of Philadelphia reveals that it had yet to learn Lincoln's correct given name.

82. The cover of this "Lincoln Quick Step" was lithographed from an 1859 Samuel M. Fassett photo by Ehrgott, Forbriger, & Company in Cincinnati. The publisher was J. Church, also of Cincinnati. The sheet music bears no copyright or composer's name.

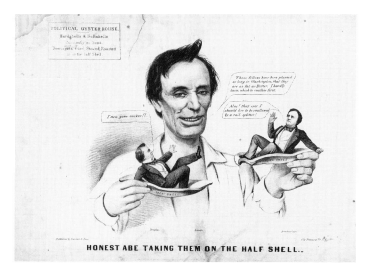

84. This Currier & Ives lithograph has Lincoln musing on which of his opponents to devour first, Douglas in the half shell labeled "soft," or Breckinridge in the one labeled "hard." The labels are meant to indicate their respective positions on the rights of slave owners in the territories. Douglas, the Illinois senator, mutters "I'm a gone sucker!!"; Illinoisans were and still are nicknamed "suckers."

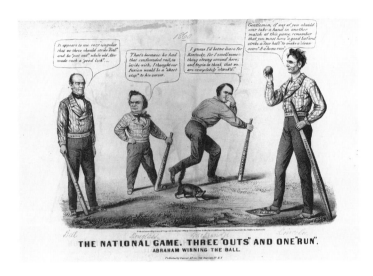

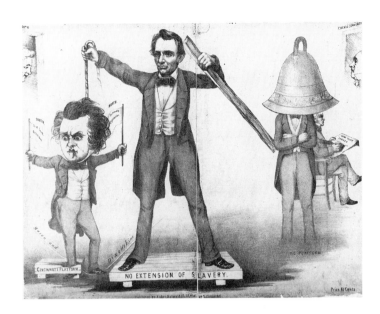

85. In this Currier & Ives lithograph the four 1860 presidential candidates appear as baseball players. Bell's bat (left) is lettered "Fusion," his belt "Union Club." Douglas's bat reads "Non Intervention," his belt "Little Giant"; while Breckinridge's mottoes are "Slavery Extension" and "Disunion Club." Lincoln stands on "Home Base" holding a bat shaped like a rail and labeled "Equal Rights and Free Territory." His belt is lettered "Wide Awake" for the Republican Wide Awakes who marched with torches and bands during the campaign of 1860.

86. Lincoln stands on the solid platform of "No Extension of Slavery" in this lithographed cartoon published by Rickey, Mallory of Cincinnati. His opponent Douglas, waving two flags ("SOUTH. Dred Scott Decision" and "NORTH. Unfriendly Legislation") stands on the Democratic platform of 1856, which held that the only solution to slavery was "popular sovereignty"—letting people in the territories decide their own domestic policies by popular vote. Another opponent, Bell, the candidate of the Constitutional Union party, stands on "No Platform" with a bell over his head.

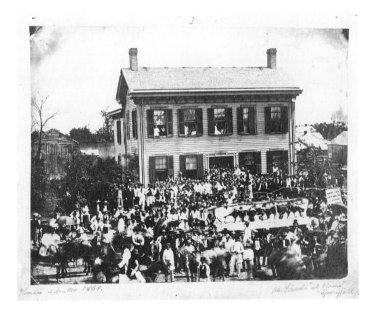

87. A large parade marched from a huge Republican rally in downtown Springfield to the Lincoln home on August 8, 1860. Lincoln, in his white linen suit, stands outside, just to the right of the front door. Mrs. Lincoln, wearing a bonnet, is inside at the far-left first-floor window. Their son, Willie, looks out from the second floor (the second window from the left), and the playful Tad is probably hiding behind a pillar somewhere. William Shaw of Chicago took the photograph, and then developed the negative in the basement of the Lincoln home.

A placard on the extreme right reads: "Wont you to let me in – Kansas." Organized as a territory in 1854, Kansas became a battleground between pro- and anti-slavery forces. Statehood was delayed by congressional maneuvering until 1861 when the territory was admitted as a free state.

88. In this lithograph the Constitutional Union candidate, Bell, looks through a telescope and reports to Douglas that the shadow of Lincoln has eclipsed the states of Connecticut, Maine, New Hampshire, Vermont, Massachusetts, New York, Pennsylvania, and Rhode Island. He says "Steph: the entir northern limb seems to eclipsed." Douglas replies, "If that is the case John we better fuse." Party leaders briefly considered fusing the two tickets, but did not get beyond preliminary discussions. Lincoln carried all the states enumerated. The lithograph was published by Rickey, Mallory of Cincinnati.

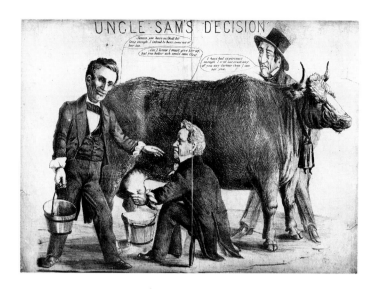

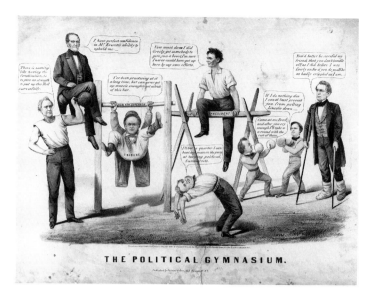

89. In *Uncle Sam's Decision* Lincoln announces to President James Buchanan that he will soon take over the task of milking the Federal cow. Buchanan replies, "Abe, I know I must give her up; but you better ask uncle sam first." Sam comments, "I have had experience enough. I will not trust any of you any farther than I can see you."

90. This Currier & Ives lithographed cartoon, *The Political Gymnasium,* shows, left to right, Edward Everett lifting his presidential candidate, John Bell, on a barbell; Horace Greeley of the *New York Tribune* trying to chin himself as the nominee for governor of New York, while Lincoln advises him from atop a rail; James Watson Webb, editor of the *New York Morning Courier* and *New York Enquirer*, doing a back flip; boxers Douglas and Breckinridge; and William H. Seward on crutches warning Bell not to fall off his perch as Seward did when he failed to win the Republican nomination for president.

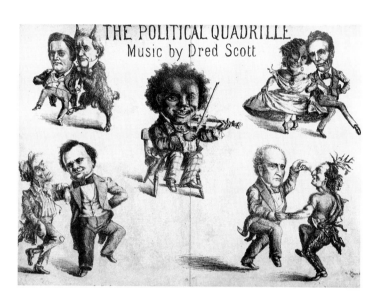

91. In this lithograph, Uncle Sam stands with Lincoln at the door of the White House and together they hold a contract signed "Un Sam" that reads: "This is to certify that I have hired A Lincoln for four years from March 1st 1861." At left, Bell, Breckinridge, and Douglas are turned away. Buchanan, the incumbent president, looks out the window in distress as he stuffs his dirty linen into a bag. The cartoon was published in 1860 by Currier & Ives.

92. In *The Political Quadrille,* published by Rickey, Mallory of Cincinnati, the four presidential candidates of 1860 are ridiculed as they dance to the fiddle music of Dred Scott: Lincoln (upper right) is dancing with a black woman; Bell (below Lincoln) with an American Indian; Breckinridge (upper left) with James Buchanan, "Old Buck," the incumbent president who has grown horns symbolizing the people's dislike of his administration; and Douglas with a tattered squatter sovereign.

Dred Scott is the black man made famous by the U.S. Supreme Court case *Dred Scott v. Sandford,* decided on March 6, 1857. The majority opinion was that a black person had no constitutional rights and that the Missouri Compromise line, which limited the extension of slavery from the Louisiana Territory above the 36 30' line, was unconstitutional. This decision was a dominant topic in the Lincoln–Douglas debates in 1858.

93. This Currier & Ives lithographed cartoon spotlights the split in the Democratic party during the campaign of 1860. At one end of the wagon, Tammany Brave, or Squatter Sovereign, attempts to drive the northern Democratic team of Stephen A. Douglas and his running mate, Herschel Johnson. At the other end, President James Buchanan, Old Buck, is trying to drive the southerner, John C. Breckinridge, and Joseph Lane in the opposite direction. Bearing down hard on the immovable wagon and about to split it in two is the locomotive, Equal Rights, with Lincoln and Hamlin aboard.

94. In the Currier & Ives lithographed cartoon *Storming the Castle,* Lincoln, rail in hand and dressed as a Wide Awake, rushes to prevent Bell, Douglas, and Breckinridge from entering the White House. "Ah! ha! Gentlemen!" Lincoln says, "you need'nt think to catch me napping; for I am a regular Wide awake." Although Douglas is trying to unlock the door with keys labeled "Regular Nomination," "Nebraska Bill," and "Non Intervention," none of them will spring the lock. Incumbent president James Buchanan lacks the strength to lift Breckinridge through the White House window.

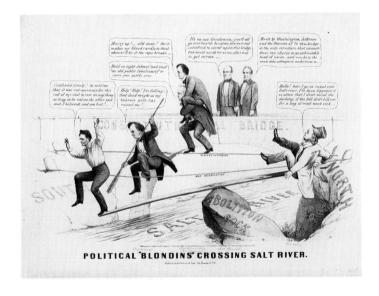

95. *Political "Blondins" Crossing Salt River* shows three of the rivals for the presidency in 1860 attempting to cross an imaginary river that separates North from South. Lincoln, with the aid of Horace Greeley, labeled "Tribune," attempts to cross on a rail that balances on "Abolition Rock." Douglas is trying to cross on the tightrope "Non Intervention" with the aid of a balance pole, but loses his balance through the weight of "Squatter Sovereignty." Breckinridge clings to the shoulders of his running mate, Joseph Lane, who also is walking a tightrope, "Slavery Extension." Bell and his running mate, Edward Everett, observe the action from "Constitutional Bridge." Blondin refers to a daredevil Frenchman, Charles Blondin, who successfully crossed Niagara Falls on a tightrope in 1859. This is a Currier & Ives lithographed cartoon.

96. *The Undecided Political Prize Fight,* an 1860 lithograph published by Rickey, Mallory of Cincinnati, shows boxer Lincoln with a black man as his second and Douglas with an old and inebriated helper.

97. *A Political Race* depicts the four 1860 presidential candidates running toward the White House. The six-foot-four Lincoln, reputedly a full foot taller than Douglas, is about to pass the rotund senator from Illinois. Breckinridge is third and Bell brings up the rear. They were running in these same positions when the popular votes were counted. This lithographed cartoon, published by Rickey, Mallory of Cincinnati, sold for ten cents.

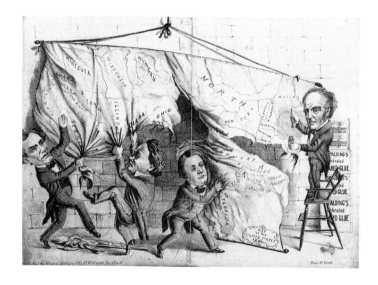

98. The 1860 presidential candidates struggle for states in this Rickey, Mallory cartoon. Lincoln and Douglas both seek to grab Ohio, Indiana, Illinois, Michigan, Wisconsin, Minnesota, Iowa, and California (Lincoln carried all eight), while Breckinridge snatches at Kentucky, Tennessee, North Carolina, South Carolina, Georgia, and Florida (he lost Tennessee and his home state of Kentucky) and Bell stands on a chair attempting to reglue the torn-away South to the North (Bell's Constitutional Union party finished last in the race).

99. This first photograph of a bearded Lincoln was taken in Chicago on November 25, 1860, by Samuel G. Alschuler. Grace Bedell may have provided the chief impetus for Lincoln to grow a beard. The eleven-year-old girl wrote the candidate from her home in Westfield, New York, on October 15, 1860, after viewing a beardless Lincoln on a campaign poster:

I have got 4 brothers and part of them will vote for you any way and if you will let your whiskers grow I will try to get the rest of them to vote for you. You would look a great deal better for your face is so thin.

Lincoln replied to Grace on October 19:

My dear little Miss.
Your very agreeable letter of the 15th. is received. I regret the necessity of saying that I have no daughters. I have three sons—one seventeen, one nine, and one seven years of age. They, with their mother, constitute my whole family.
As to the whiskers, never having worn any, do you not think people would call it a piece of silly affection if I were to begin it now?
Your very sincere well-wisher
A. Lincoln.

By mid-November Lincoln was letting his beard grow and was fully bearded when he boarded the train in Springfield on February 11, 1861, for his inauguration in Washington. When his train stopped in Westfield, he called for the little girl. She made her way through the crowd, and after being helped to the platform, was kissed by the president-elect.

100. This portrait of Lincoln in late 1860 is one of two Lincolns painted by Jesse Atwood of Philadelphia. Atwood was in Springfield during October and November 1860, and Lincoln sat for him in an improvised office made available in the Illinois Capitol. This is the first known painting of Lincoln with a beard, and it is doubtful that the beard was as fully grown as the artist painted it.

Many of the artists who journeyed to Springfield to paint Lincoln after his nomination were executing commissions for Republican patrons and lithographic publishers, but there is no information that Atwood was so employed. The artist's granddaughter, Clara V. Fisher, said that Atwood also painted portraits of other presidents, including John Quincy Adams, Zachary Taylor, and Franklin Pierce.

This portrait remained in the Atwood family until about 1900, when Samuel Pennypacker, later governor of Pennsylvania, acquired it. J. E. Barr of Philadelphia purchased it from the Pennypacker estate, and later it went first to J. W. Young, a Chicago art dealer, and then to Indiana University. It is now in The Lilly Library..

101. Mary Lincoln and her two younger sons were photographed in Springfield in the fall of 1860 at the gallery of Preston Butler. William Wallace "Willie" Lincoln strikes a Napoleon pose at the left, while Thomas "Tad" Lincoln holds his mother's hand.

Lincoln married Mary Ann Todd, from Lexington, Kentucky, in Springfield on November 4, 1842. Much has been written about their courtship, broken engagement, reconciliation, and marriage, as well as the differences in their social and cultural backgrounds. They based their marriage on love, trust, mutual respect, and tolerance, and they made it work. They formed a loving and caring family. Mary and Abraham both had emotional problems. He was on the judicial circuit several months of the year and was not always the most thoughtful of husbands.

The first of their four sons, Robert Todd Lincoln, named for his maternal grandfather, was born at the Globe Tavern in Springfield on August 1, 1843. The only son of the Lincolns to reach maturity, he died in 1926. The other three sons were born at the Lincoln home at Eighth and Jackson streets in Springfield. Edward Baker, called Eddie after a close Lincoln associate, was born on March 10, 1846. Eddie died at the Lincoln home on February 1, 1850. Willie Lincoln, named after Dr. William Wallace (husband of Mary's sister, Frances Todd Wallace), was born on December 21, 1850, and died at the White House on February 20, 1862. Tad Lincoln was born on April 4, 1853, and was named for his paternal grandfather. He died on July 15, 1871, probably of cardiopulmonary problems, about two months after he and his mother returned from an extended trip to Europe. They were residing in a Chicago hotel, the Clifton House, at the time of his death.

102. Thomas "Tad" Lincoln, age seven, posed for a photographer in Springfield in 1860.

103. William Wallace "Willie" Lincoln posed for the photographer at age ten in Springfield in 1860.

104. This unusual photograph of Mary Todd Lincoln is in the form of a carte-de-visite. It bears no imprint of a photographer or seller and no copyright notice.

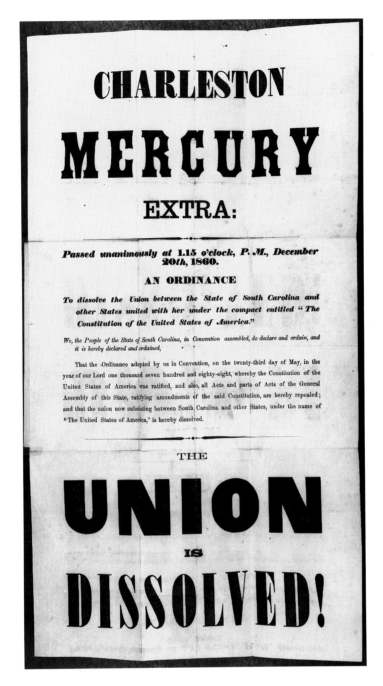

Departure for Washington; First Administration; Civil War
(Nos. 105–154)

105. South Carolina warned that it would secede from the Union if Lincoln was elected. When the news of his election victory reached the state, the legislature by unanimous vote called for a state convention, which met at Columbia. On December 20, 1860, an ordinance was passed "To dissolve the Union between the State of South Carolina and other States united with her under the compact entitled 'The Constitution of the United States of America.'" States were sovereign, went the argument, and secession was justified because of the North's long attack on slavery and the election of a president whose opinions and purposes were hostile to slavery.

Between January 9 and February 1, 1861, six other states— Mississippi, Florida, Alabama, Georgia, Louisiana, and Texas—followed South Carolina's lead. On February 4, delegates from the seceding states met in Montgomery, Alabama, and by February 9 had framed a constitution, organized a provisional government, and elected Jefferson Davis as provisional president of the Confederate States of America.

106. The Reuben Moore house, built in the 1850s, was the home of Sarah Bush Johnston Lincoln's daughter, Matilda Johnston Hall Moore, Lincoln's stepsister. Sarah Lincoln was staying with her widowed daughter (Matilda's second husband, Reuben, had died in 1859) when the president-elect came to visit her in this Coles County home in eastern Illinois on January 31, 1861, before he left for Washington. He also visited family members who lived in the area and went to visit the grave of his father, Thomas Lincoln, in the nearby Shiloh Cemetery. That evening he returned to Charleston with Sarah, and they said their farewells the next morning. The Moore Home, now a satellite of the Lincoln Log Cabin State Historic Site, is administered by the Illinois Historic Preservation Agency.

107. Sarah Bush Johnston Lincoln, stepmother of Abraham Lincoln, is shown in a photograph taken after her stepson was assassinated. Thomas Lincoln married the widowed Sarah or "Sally" on December 2, 1819, in Elizabethtown, Kentucky. The three children from her first marriage, Elizabeth, Matilda, and John, became part of the Lincoln family. Sally brought many innovations with her to southern Indiana and greatly improved the facilities of the Lincoln cabin, which now housed eight people. One of her daughters said: "When father and mother married he had children and we went to live with her, and she took the children and mixed us all up together like hasty pudding, and has not known us apart since." Sally encouraged the teenage Lincoln to read and study. As Lincoln wrote in his third-person autobiography, "She proved a good and kind mother to him." He always referred to her as "mother" and she called him "Abe." He treated her with the utmost love and respect, frequently visited her Coles County home after moving to Springfield, and protected her from her avaricious son, John D. Johnston. She died in 1869 at age eighty-one and is buried next to her husband, Thomas, in the Shiloh Cemetery near the Lincoln homestead south of Charleston, Illinois.

PRESIDENT LINCOLN'S
FAREWELL ADDRESS

TO HIS OLD NEIGHBORS,

SPRINGFIELD, FEBRUARY 12, 1861.

My Friends.

No one not in my position can appreciate the sadness I feel at this parting. To this people I owe all that I am. Here I have lived more than a quarter of a century; here my children were born, and here one of them lies buried. I know not how soon I shall see you again. A duty devolves upon me which is, perhaps, greater than that which has devolved upon any other man since the days of Washington. He never would have succeeded except for the aid of Divine Providence, upon which he at all times relied. I feel that I cannot succeed without the same Divine aid which sustained him, and on the same Almighty Being I place my reliance for support, and I hope you, my friends, will all pray that I may receive that Divine assistance without which I cannot succeed, but with which success is certain. Again I bid you an affectionate farewell.

108. President-elect Lincoln started his circuitous journey to Washington on the morning of February 11, 1861, from the Great Western Railroad depot in Springfield. A crowd estimated at one thousand or more gathered to witness the departure. In response to the crowd's wishes, he spoke extemporaneously from the rear platform of the train. Later he and John G. Nicolay, his secretary, wrote out his farewell remarks at the request of a newspaper reporter. This version is one of the three, which differ only slightly.

109. Lincoln gave his farewell here at the Great Western Railroad passenger station on February 11, 1861. It stands on Monroe Street between Ninth and Tenth streets in Springfield and now serves as a museum. This photograph was taken in 1994.

110. This bronze statue, the work of Andrew O'Connor, stands at the end of Springfield's Capitol Avenue before the east entrance of the Illinois Statehouse. It was dedicated on October 6, 1918, as part of the centenary celebration marking the first meeting of the Illinois General Assembly. The artist apparently intended to depict Lincoln as he was leaving Springfield for Washington on February 11, 1861; his departing remarks are inscribed on the massive stone slab behind the statue. If so, he should have portrayed Lincoln with a full-grown beard.

111, 112. President Lincoln's secretaries, John Milton Hay (*left*) and John George Nicolay (*right*). Friends before their appointments, the two men started to work for Lincoln in Springfield, Nicolay shortly after Lincoln was nominated for the presidency, Hay after Lincoln was elected. Both accompanied the president-elect on his journey to Washington for the inauguration. They served Lincoln in a variety of ways: screening visitors, sorting mail, writing letters for Lincoln's signature, and preparing daily news summaries. Lincoln used both of them on special missions far beyond Washington. Both roomed in the White House but took meals in town. The youthful secretaries (Nicolay was twenty-eight and Hay twen-

ty-one when they signed on) fondly termed Lincoln "Tycoon" or the "Ancient," but only to each other. Hay sometimes admiringly referred to Lincoln as the "backwoods Jupiter." Both served Lincoln until his death.

Following their service in the White House, they served in diplomatic posts and other positions. Their ten-volume *Abraham Lincoln: A History,* published in 1890, in book form, was fifteen years in preparation. They used the Lincoln Papers, now in the Library of Congress, but then in the custody of Robert Todd Lincoln, who demanded some changes in the text. From October 1886 to January 1890 about half of the biography appeared in serial form in the *Century Magazine*.

113. President-elect Lincoln reached Washington on February 23, 1861, after a twelve-day, seven-state, circuitous journey through Indianapolis, Cincinnati, Columbus, Pittsburgh, Cleveland, Buffalo, Albany, New York City, Philadelphia, Harrisburg, and Baltimore, with several stops in between. The journey was conceived to introduce him to thousands of citizens in the curious and anxious nation. In the capital he was soon in the studio of Mathew B. Brady, sitting for a series of photographs. During the posing he kept his right hand closed (as here) or out of sight; it was swollen as a result of many handshakes on his journey.

114. In this Brady photograph taken on the same visit as the preceding one the president-elect was concerned about the time. He has just taken his watch from his vest pocket and holds it; the case is still open in his right hand.

115. From his election on November 6, 1860, until his inauguration on March 4, 1861, president-elect Lincoln did not comment publicly on the dissolution of the Union. Even though seven southern states seceded, framed a constitution, and formed a provisional confederate government, Lincoln issued no statement, presented no program, and gave not the slightest hint of the course of action he would take once in office. In retrospect, it appears that he overestimated Union strength and underrated dissolution sentiment then prevailing. He certainly did not realize that many southerners were more loyal to their state than to the Union.

Lincoln's first Inaugural Address was notable, containing words conciliatory toward the South:

> *I have no purpose directly or indirectly to interfere with the institution of slavery in the states where it exists. I believe I have no lawful right to do so, and have no inclination to do so.*

But he also expressed his firm belief that "no state upon its own mere motion can lawfully get out of the Union." His concluding words, as printed in the *Daily Chicago Post*'s extra edition on the day they were delivered:

> *I am loth to close; we are not enemies but friends. We must not be enemies, though passion may have strained, it must not break our bodies of action.*
>
> *The mystic cords of memory stretched from every battle field and patriotic grave to every living hea[r]t and hearthstone all over this broad land, will yet swell the chorus of the Union when again touched, as surely they will be, by the better angels of our nature.*

116. The Capitol was undergoing major renovation on the morning of Lincoln's first inauguration, March 4, 1861. The original dome had been removed, and the base of the new cast-iron dome, topped by scaffolding and a crane, is shown mounted on the old sandstone. Work continued on the building during the Civil War. The colossal Statue of Freedom was finally placed on the lantern of the dome on December 2, 1863.

117. This shows the White House as it appeared during the Lincoln Administration.

118. This engraving of Lincoln and his first cabinet was published by J. C. Buttre of New York and entered for copyright in 1862.

Lincoln had selected only two members of his seven-man cabinet before reaching Washington on February 23, 1861: William Henry Seward (*top center*), former governor of New York and the leading candidate for the Republican nomination for president in 1860, for Secretary of State and Edward Bates of Missouri (*bottom left*) for Attorney General. Caleb Blood Smith (*top left*), an Indianapolis lawyer, was appointed to head the Interior Department. Simon Cameron, Pennsylvania's Senator, was appointed as Secretary of War in spite of many protests from his political enemies both in and out of Pennsylvania. Cameron was dismissed on January 18, 1862, and replaced by Edwin McMasters Stanton. It is Stanton who is pictured in this engraving (*center right*). Montgomery Blair (*bottom right*), a Republican leader from Maryland, became Postmaster General. Gideon Welles (*center left*), organizer of the Republican party in Connecticut and a newspaper editor, was appointed Secretary of the Navy. Salmon Portland Chase (*top right*), former governor of Ohio, became Secretary of the Treasury. Also shown in the engraving is Vice-President Hannibal Hamlin (*bottom center*).

119. Alonzo Weeks designed this composite of Lincoln's cabinet from photographs taken by Mathew B. Brady and Company. It was entered for copyright in 1864. William H. Seward and Gideon Welles served Lincoln from the beginning of his administration. William Dennison (*bottom right*) replaced Blair as Postmaster General on October 1, 1864. John Palmer Usher (*bottom left*), a Terre Haute, Indiana, lawyer, replaced Caleb B. Smith as Secretary of the Interior on January 8, 1863. James Speed (*bottom center*), a Kentucky lawyer and brother of Lincoln's best friend, Joshua Speed, replaced Edward Bates as Attorney General on December 5, 1864. Hugh McCulloch (*top right*), a banker from Fort Wayne, Indiana, became Secretary of the Treasury on March 9, 1865.

125, 126. These two tributes in sheet music demonstrate the nation's concern for and the popularity of young Colonel Ellsworth. The cover for the "Monody" is in color; the funeral march was composed by J. D. Beckel. The "Requiem March," with a cover lithographed by Ed. Mendel of Chicago, was composed by A. J. Vaas for a special memorial ceremony at Bryan Hall in Chicago on June 2, 1861.

Ellsworth had read law in Lincoln's law office in Springfield for a short time in 1860. The Lincolns, including the two younger boys, had developed a fondness for him, and he had accompanied the president-elect on his inaugural trip to Washington. His death deeply touched the president and his family, and Lincoln wrote the young man's parents the following letter:

> My dear Sir and Madam, In the untimely loss of your noble son, our affliction here, is scarcely less than your own. So much of promised usefulness to one's country, and of bright hopes for one's self and friends, have rarely been so suddenly dashed, as in his fall. In size, in years, and in youthful appearance, a boy only, his power to command men, was surpassingly great. This power, combined with a fine intel-

lect, an indomitable energy, and a taste altogether military, constituted in him, as seemed to me, the best natural talent, in that department, I ever knew. And yet he was singularly modest and deferential in social intercourse. My acquaintance with him began less than two years ago; yet through the latter half of the intervening period, it was as intimate as the disparity of our ages, and my engrossing engagements, would permit. To me, he appeared to have no indulgences or pastimes; and I have never heard him utter a profane or an intemperate word. What was conclusive of his good heart, he never forgot his parents. The honors he labored for so laudably, and, in the sad end, so gallantly gave his life, he meant for them, no less than for himself.

> In the hope that it may be no intrusion upon the sacredness of your sorrow, I have ventured to address you this tribute to the memory of my young friend, and your brave and early fallen child.

> May God give you that consolation which is beyond all earthly power.

> Sincerely your friend in a common affliction—
> A. Lincoln

127, 128. The Lincolns' oldest son, Robert Todd Lincoln (1843–1926), studied at Illinois State University, a college preparatory school, in Springfield and Phillips Exeter Academy in New Hampshire. He entered Harvard University in 1860 and graduated in 1864, ranking in the top third of his class. The dates of these two photographs of Robert Todd are unknown.

Through the influence of his father, he was appointed captain on General Ulysses S. Grant's staff and was present at General Robert E. Lee's surrender to Grant on April 9, 1865, at Appomattox Court House. After studying law in Chicago,

he was admitted to the bar in 1867. He married Mary Eunice Harlan in 1868, and they had three children: Mary (born 1869), Abraham "Jack" (1873), and Jesse Harlan (1875).

He served as Secretary of War under Presidents Garfield and Arthur and was appointed Minister to England by President Benjamin Harrison in 1889. After returning from England in 1893, he continued his legal work and in 1897 became president of the Pullman Company. He retired in 1911 and died on July 26, 1926, at his summer house in Manchester, Vermont. He is buried at the Arlington National Cemetery in Virginia.

129. This 1861 photograph of Mary Todd Lincoln was taken at the Washington or New York studio of Mathew B. Brady. The dress she wears is now in the Illinois Historical Library in Springfield, Illinois.

130. William Wallace "Willie" (standing) and Thomas "Tad" Lincoln pose with Lockwood Todd, Mary Lincoln's cousin, at Mathew Brady's Washington gallery in 1861.

131. Thomas "Tad" Lincoln poses in his Union officer's uniform. An undisciplined little rascal, Tad had the run of the entire White House, including his father's office when affairs of state were being discussed. After the death of his brother Willie in 1862, the Lincolns poured more and more affection on their youngest son, who spoke with a slight lisp. After Lincoln's assassination, Tad became his mother's constant companion. He received no formal education while living in the White House but was in school in Chicago from 1866 to 1868, and attended a boarding school in Frankfurt, Germany, from 1868 to 1870. He died in Chicago on July 15, 1871, probably of cardiopulmonary problems.

The uniform in which Tad was photographed was a gift from Secretary of War Edwin M. Stanton. Tad was fond of playing soldier, and Stanton had commissioned him a lieutenant. One night, using his fictitious rank, Tad mustered the White House staff, dismissed the regular staff guard, and ordered cooks and doormen to stand sentry duty. But Tad soon fell asleep, and his father dismissed the fake guards and tenderly carried his warrior son to bed.

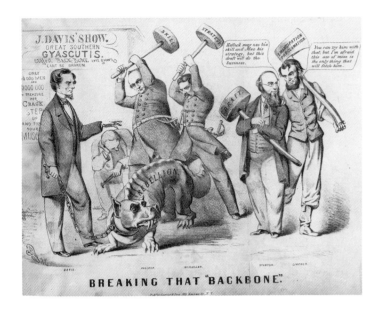

132. This Currier & Ives lithograph, *Breaking That "Backbone,"* was published in 1862 and signed by artist Ben Day. Henry W. Halleck, General-in-Chief, and General George McClellan flail away but cannot mount a military victory sufficient to break the back of the rebellion. Edwin M. Stanton, Lincoln's second Secretary of War, thinks a new draft of soldiers will bring victories, while Lincoln believes the Emancipation Proclamation will break the rebellion.

134. George Frederick Root, music publisher, composer, and teacher of music in Chicago, wrote both the words and music to this ballad, "The Battle Cry of Freedom," in July 1862. It became one of the most popular songs of the Civil War, on both the home and the military front. One young soldier wrote that "the tune put as much spirit and cheer into the Army as a splendid victory." Long after the Civil War, the refrain "Yes, we'll rally round the flag, boys, we'll rally once again, shouting the battle cry of Freedom" could bring tears to the eyes of aging Union veterans. An estimated 700,000 copies of the sheet music were printed between 1862 and 1865.

133. This photograph of Mary Lincoln taken by Mathew B. Brady in Washington is from a visiting card in the Robert Coster Collection. It was entered for copyright in 1862 in the District of Columbia.

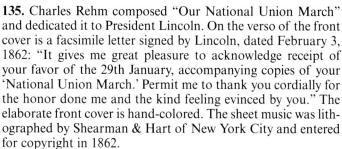

135. Charles Rehm composed "Our National Union March" and dedicated it to President Lincoln. On the verso of the front cover is a facsimile letter signed by Lincoln, dated February 3, 1862: "It gives me great pleasure to acknowledge receipt of your favor of the 29th January, accompanying copies of your 'National Union March.' Permit me to thank you cordially for the honor done me and the kind feeling evinced by you." The elaborate front cover is hand-colored. The sheet music was lithographed by Shearman & Hart of New York City and entered for copyright in 1862.

136, 137. On July 1, 1862, President Lincoln called for 300,000 volunteers to serve in the Union forces for three years, or until the end of the war. In response, James Sloan Gibbons, New York banker, sent a poem to the *New York Evening Post*, which published it without indicating who wrote it. Soon set to music, "We are Coming Father Abra'am" became a very popular Civil War song:

> We are coming Father Abra'am, three hundred thousand more,
> From Mississippi's winding stream and from New England's shore;
> We leave our plows and workshops, our wives and children dear,
> With hearts too full for utterance, with but a silent tear;
> We dare not look behind us, but steadfastly before,
> We are coming Father Abra'am, three hundred thousand more!

Six months after the initial publication, at least twenty editions, with music by various composers, had been published. Lincoln's first name was spelled four different ways: Abra'am, Abraam, Abram, and Abraham. All six editions in these two photographs were entered for copyright in 1862. They have the same lyrics, except that three of them substitute "600,000 more" for "300,000 more." None carries the name of Gibbons as author of the lyrics. Some music publishers gave credit for the words to poet William Cullen Bryant, editor of the *Evening Post*, but he disavowed authorship. Estimates are that two million copies of the various editions circulated.

138. "President Lincoln's Grand March," composed by F. B. Helmsmuller, leader of the New York Twenty-Second Regimental Band, was entered for copyright in 1862. The elaborate front cover was hand-colored.

139. President Lincoln visits General George Brinton McClellan at Antietam in this photograph taken by Alexander Gardner for Mathew Brady on October 3, 1862. McClellan, Commander of the Army of the Potomac, had stopped the Confederate invasion of Maryland at the Battle of Antietam near Sharpsburg, Maryland, on September 17, 1862, but had failed to use his reserves and follow up the battle. Lincoln's visit, unannounced, was meant to persuade the General to take the offensive at once. Confederate General Robert E. Lee was in the Shenandoah Valley, far from Richmond, and not firmly based. When McClellan finally moved, six weeks after Antietam, it was too late; his advantage was gone. On November 7, Lincoln removed McClellan from his command and appointed Major General Ambrose E. Burnside to succeed him.

140. Lincoln stands at Antietam on October 2 or 3, 1862, between Major General John A. McClernand (right) and Allan Pinkerton, chief of the Secret Service. The man sitting on the ground holding up the number 7949 was the photographer Alexander Gardner's helper.

BY THE PRESIDENT OF THE UNITED STATES OF AMERICA.

A Proclamation.

Whereas, on the twenty-second day of September, in the year of our Lord one thousand eight hundred and sixty-two, a proclamation was issued by the President of the United States, containing, among other things, the following, to wit:

"That on the first day of January, in the year of our Lord one thousand eight hundred and sixty-three, all persons held as slaves within any State or designated part of a State, the people whereof shall then be in rebellion against the United States, shall be then, thenceforward, and forever, free; and the Executive government of the United States, including the military and naval authority thereof, will recognize and maintain the freedom of such persons, and will do no act or acts to repress such persons, or any of them, in any efforts they may make for their actual freedom.

"That the Executive will, on the first day of January aforesaid, by proclamation, designate the States and parts of States, if any, in which the people thereof, respectively, shall then be in rebellion against the United States; and the fact that any State, or the people thereof, shall on that day be in good faith represented in the Congress of the United States, by members chosen thereto at elections wherein a majority of the qualified voters of such State shall have participated, shall, in the absence of strong countervailing testimony, be deemed conclusive evidence that such State, and the people thereof, are not then in rebellion against the United States."

Now, therefore, I, ABRAHAM LINCOLN, PRESIDENT OF THE UNITED STATES, by virtue of the power in me vested as commander-in-chief of the army and navy of the United States, in time of actual armed rebellion against the authority and government of the United States, and as a fit and necessary war measure for suppressing said rebellion, do, on this first day of January, in the year of our Lord one thousand eight hundred and sixty-three, and in accordance with my purpose so to do, publicly proclaimed for the full period of one hundred days from the day first above mentioned, order and designate as the States and parts of States wherein the people thereof, respectively, are this day in rebellion against the United States, the following, to wit: ARKANSAS, TEXAS, LOUISIANA, (except the Parishes of St. Bernard, Plaquemines, Jefferson, St. John, St. Charles, St. James, Ascension, Assumption, Terre Bonne, Lafourche, St. Mary, St. Martin, and Orleans, including the City of New Orleans,) MISSISSIPPI, ALABAMA, FLORIDA, GEORGIA, SOUTH CAROLINA, NORTH CAROLINA, AND VIRGINIA, (except the forty-eight counties designated as West Virginia, and also the counties of Berkeley, Accomac, Northampton, Elizabeth City, York, Princess Ann, and Norfolk, including the cities of Norfolk and Portsmouth,) and which excepted parts are for the present left precisely as if this proclamation were not issued.

And by virtue of the power and for the purpose aforesaid, I do order and declare that all persons held as slaves within said designated States and parts of States are and henceforward shall be free; and that the Executive government of the United States, including the military and naval authorities thereof, will recognize and maintain the freedom of said persons.

And I hereby enjoin upon the people so declared to be free to abstain from all violence, unless in necessary self-defence; and I recommend to them that, in all cases when allowed, they labor faithfully for reasonable wages.

And I further declare and make known that such persons, of suitable condition, will be received into the armed service of the United States, to garrison forts, positions, stations, and other places, and to man vessels of all sorts in said service.

And upon this act, sincerely believed to be an act of justice warranted by the Constitution upon military necessity, I invoke the considerate judgment of mankind and the gracious favor of Almighty God.

In witness whereof I have hereunto set my hand and caused the seal of the United States to be affixed.

[L. S.]   Done at the CITY OF WASHINGTON this first day of January, in the year of our Lord one thousand eight hundred and sixty-three, and of the Independence of the United States of America the eighty-seventh.

By the President:

Abraham Lincoln

Willm H Seward   *Secretary of State.*

A true copy, with the autograph signatures of the President and the Secretary of State.

Jno. G. Nicolay
Priv. Sec. to the President.

141. (*Opposite*) The Emancipation Proclamation, signed on January 1, 1863, was probably the most important document of Lincoln's presidency. Great pressure had been exerted on Lincoln by abolitionists and members of Congress to strike a blow against slavery as the evil that had caused the Civil War. Lincoln had expressed his feelings on the subject to Horace Greeley, editor of the *New York Tribune* and his constant critic, on August 22, 1862:

> *My paramount object in this struggle is to save the Union, and is not either to save or destroy slavery. If I could save the Union without freeing any slave I would do it, and if I could do it by freeing all the slaves I would do it; and if I could save it by freeing some and leaving others alone I would also do that. What I do about slavery, and the colored race, I do because I believe it helps to save the Union . . .*

Eventually Lincoln came to believe that abolition of slavery would cripple the economic system of the Confederacy and thus could be justified as a war measure. On September 23, 1862, he issued a preliminary proclamation and announced it was to be followed three months later by the official proclamation freeing all slaves in areas still in rebellion.

The Proclamation in 1863 did not settle the slavery issue. In practice the edict freed few slaves, but it was a step toward freedom for all blacks. Lincoln and many members of the Republican party felt that the Proclamation was of dubious legality, and Lincoln favored a constitutional amendment abolishing slavery. The future Thirteenth Amendment to the Constitution passed in the U.S. Senate in 1864 but was held up in the House until January 31, 1865, when Lincoln used the force of his office and his control of patronage to ensure passage. Eight months after Lincoln's assassination, in December 1865, it was finally ratified by three-fourths of the states. Eight of the ratifying states were former members of the Confederacy: Virginia, Tennessee, Arkansas, South Carolina, Alabama, North Carolina, Georgia, and Louisiana.

142. This satirical etching of Lincoln writing the Emancipation Proclamation was the work of Adalbert John Volch, a native of Bavaria and a Baltimore dentist and caricaturist. Volch sympathized with the South (historians labeled him a copperhead) and published several works favorable to the Confederacy. In this etching, finished in 1862, Lincoln's foot rests on a bound copy of the Constitution and the devil's inkpot furnishes ink for his writing. On the wall hangs a portrait of John Brown, labeled "St. Ossawotamie," and a depiction of rioting and bloodshed in "St. Domingo" following the abolition of slavery there.

UNIVERSAL ADVICE TO ABRAHAM.
DROP 'EM!

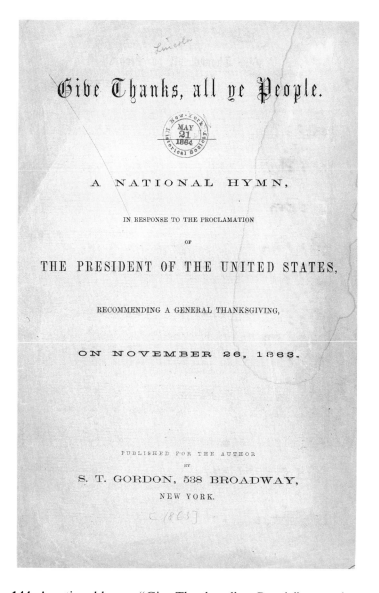

143. On January 10, 1863, *Harper's Weekly* published this cartoon, *Universal Advice to Abraham. Drop 'Em!* Secretary of War Edwin Stanton, with beard and eyeglasses, and Henry W. Halleck, General-in-Chief, came under fire from the press and many in the military. Lincoln did not drop Stanton, who served him faithfully and well, but Halleck was demoted to Chief of Staff of the Army in 1864, a position of minor importance compared to his former office.

144. A national hymn, "Give Thanks, all ye People" was written in response to President Lincoln's proclamation of a day of giving thanks. Thanksgiving is the oldest holiday observed in the United States, a heritage from early English settlers who celebrated the autumnal harvest with feasts and entertainment. The annual nationwide observance began with Lincoln's proclamation in 1863. All presidents followed Lincoln's example and issued proclamations for a day of thanksgiving. Except for two deviations, the last Thursday in November became the traditional day for Thanksgiving until 1939.

President Franklin D. Roosevelt altered the day in 1939, following pressure by the National Retail Goods Association. He moved the date forward to November 23, 1939, thus allowing twenty-four shopping days between Thanksgiving and Christmas. The nation was jolted by this action and a hail of rhetoric, plus a field day for cartoonists and humorists, followed the announcement of "Franksgiving." Congress pacified the traditionalists by a joint resolution establishing the fourth Thursday in November as Thanksgiving. The joint resolution became Public Law 379 on December 26, 1941.

Sarah Josepha Hale, editor of *Godey's Lady's Book*, had urged Lincoln to act. John G. Nicolay, secretary to Lincoln, stated that the proclamation was written by William H. Seward. Dated October 3, 1863, it concludes: "I do therefore invite my fellow citizens in every part of the United States, and also those who are at sea and those who are sojourning in foreign lands, to set apart and observe the last Thursday of November next, as a day of Thanksgiving and Praise to our Beneficent Father who dwelleth in the Heavens."

145. The monumental battle between the armies of the Union and the Confederacy at Gettysburg, Pennsylvania, between July 1 and July 3, 1863, took an extremely heavy toll in lives and injuries on both sides. Many of those who fell in the three-day battle had been hastily and inadequately buried. The result was a grisly sight, with bodies exposed and hogs uprooting the shallow graves. Union pride led to the formation of an interstate commission to rebury the dead in appropriate surroundings. William Saunders, a rural architect employed by the U.S. Department of Agriculture, was retained to plan the layout of the cemetery. He aligned the graves by state and was careful to avoid giving preferential treatment to any one state.

This "Order of Procession for the Inauguration of the National Cemetery at Gettysburg, Pa." is a memento of the dedication on November 19, 1863, which attracted a huge crowd. State governors with their delegations attended, as did members of many civic and fraternal organizations and a group of foreign diplomats. Military units and regimental bands added color to the occasion. Edward Everett, orator, statesman, scholar, and running mate of presidential candidate John Bell in the 1860 election, was the principal speaker. He spoke for two hours from memory, analyzing the Battle of Gettysburg in detail.

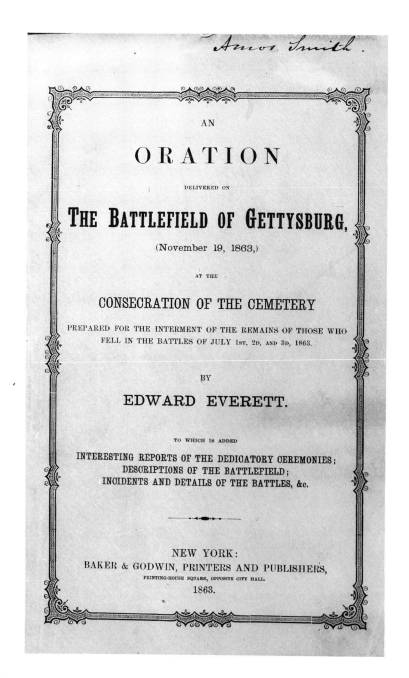

Amos Smith.

AN
ORATION

DELIVERED ON

THE BATTLEFIELD OF GETTYSBURG,

(November 19, 1863,)

AT THE

CONSECRATION OF THE CEMETERY

PREPARED FOR THE INTERMENT OF THE REMAINS OF THOSE WHO
FELL IN THE BATTLES OF JULY 1ST, 2D, AND 3D, 1863.

BY

EDWARD EVERETT.

TO WHICH IS ADDED

INTERESTING REPORTS OF THE DEDICATORY CEREMONIES;
DESCRIPTIONS OF THE BATTLEFIELD;
INCIDENTS AND DETAILS OF THE BATTLES, &c.

NEW YORK:
BAKER & GODWIN, PRINTERS AND PUBLISHERS,
PRINTING-HOUSE SQUARE, OPPOSITE CITY HALL.
1863.

---

146. In this pamphlet recording the events of the dedication of the cemetery at Gettysburg, President Lincoln's remarks appear on page forty, following the text of Edward Everett's oration. Lincoln was invited to make "a few appropriate remarks" after Everett's speech. Although his invitation came late, and his son was ill in the White House, he accepted promptly. He could not forego an opportunity to mingle with governors and other political heavyweights to get firsthand readings on the political situations. But his primary purpose at Gettysburg was to explain the meaning of the war and why it had to be successfully concluded.

Lincoln spoke for less than three minutes, but his words gave lasting meaning to the lives sacrificed in the battle. Many superlatives have been used to describe the *Gettysburg Address*, and the sentiments endure:

Four score and seven years ago our fathers brought forth upon this continent, a new nation, conceived in Liberty, and dedicated to the proposition that all men are created equal.

Now we are engaged in a great civil war, testing whether that nation, or any nation so conceived and so dedicated, can long endure. We are met on a great battle-field of that war. We have come to dedicate a portion of that field, as a final resting place for those who here gave their lives that that nation might live. It is altogether fitting and proper that we should do this.

But, in a larger sense, we cannot dedicate—we cannot consecrate—we cannot hallow—this ground. The brave men, living and dead, who struggled here, have consecrated it, far above our poor power to add or detract. The world will little note, nor long remember what we say here, but it can never forget what they did here. It is for us the living, rather, to be dedicated here to the unfinished work which they who fought here have thus far so nobly advanced. It is rather for us to be here dedicated to the great task remaining before us—that from these honored dead we take increased devotion to that cause for which they gave the last full measure of devotion—that we here highly resolve that these dead shall not have died in vain—that this nation, under God, shall have a new birth of freedom—and that government of the people, by the people, for the people, shall not perish from the earth.

147. The gate to Gettysburg National Cemetery was photographed in 1863.

148. Part of the crowd near the speaker's platform is shown in this photograph taken during the dedication ceremonies of the cemetery at Gettysburg on November 19, 1863. The crowd was estimated to total nearly twenty thousand.

149, 150. President and Mrs. Lincoln never posed for a photograph or a portrait together. These companion portraits were painted by Francis Bicknell Carpenter while he was residing in the White House (February 4 to the end of July 1864) and painting his *First Reading of the Emancipation Proclamation.*

The painting of the president measures 10 3/4 by 9 inches, that of Mrs. Lincoln 9 by 7 inches. The portraits were a gift to The Lilly Library by George A. Ball of Muncie, Indiana, who served as a Trustee of Indiana University from 1919 to 1938.

151. This photograph of President Lincoln was taken by Wenderoth and Taylor, a Philadelphia firm, at the White House in 1864.

152. In this Brady Gallery photograph of President Lincoln with his son Tad, taken on February 9, 1864, Lincoln wears spectacles, a rare occurrence when he was being photographed.

153. Anthony Berger took this photograph of Lincoln at the Brady Gallery on February 9, 1864. The oval portrait of Lincoln engraved on the five-dollar bill was adapted from this photograph.

154. This photograph of Mary Lincoln, a carte-de-visite, was entered for copyright in 1865 by E. and H. T. Anthony of New York, a firm advertised as "Manufacturers of the Best Photographic Albums." The Lilly Library acquired it from Robert Coster. The photograph may have been taken earlier than 1865, for Mrs. Lincoln is wearing mourning attire following the death of her son, Willie. Some authorities date the photograph to autumn 1863.

Second Presidential Campaign; Second Administration
(Nos. 155–190)

155. (*Opposite*) *The Platforms*, financed by the Union Republican party, summarizes the "Points of Difference" between the Union and Democratic parties in 1864.

As the 1864 election grew near, Lincoln was certain of the nomination because he and his workers could use the patronage system to accomplish that goal. There were other aspirers (notably Salmon P. Chase, Lincoln's Secretary of the Treasury), but they did not possess enough appeal to be nominated. Pro-Lincoln delegates were in the majority when the Republicans met in Baltimore on June 7. They called themselves the Union party to emphasize their goal of saving the Union. Lincoln was nominated on the first ballot. For vice-president they selected Andrew Johnson, a southern Unionist Democrat and military governor of Tennessee, making the ticket veritably a "union."

The platform of the Union party approved "the determination of the Government of the United States not to compromise with rebels, nor to offer any terms of peace except such as may be based upon an 'unconditional surrender' of their hostility and a return to their just allegiance to the Constitution and laws of the United States. . . ." The platform also called for an amendment to the Constitution abolishing slavery, paid respects to the Union troops and promised provision for those who were disabled, and approved the Emancipation Proclamation. Immigrants were encouraged to come to the United States as "the asylum of the oppressed of all nations." The people of California and Oregon were promised the "speedy construction of a Railroad to the Pacific." The eleventh plank warned European governments, in diplomatic vernacular, to stay out of "the western continent."

The Democratic National Convention met in Chicago on August 29, 1864, and nominated General George B. McClellan for president and George H. Pendleton as his running mate. The candidate and the platform were diametrically different. The platform demanded that the war be stopped "to the end that at the earliest practicable moment peace may be restored on the basis of the Federal Union of the States." McClellan repudiated this peace platform of the party's radical wing and declared that successful prosecution of the war was the only road to peace.

Lincoln was pessimistic about his chances of winning a second term. President Andrew Jackson had been the last president to serve two terms. On August 23, Lincoln wrote the following memorandum, folded and sealed it, and asked members of his Cabinet to sign, without knowing its content:

> *This morning, as for some days past, it seems exceedingly probable that this Administration will not be re-elected. Then it will be my duty to cooperate with the President elect, as to save the Union between the election and the inauguration; as he will have secured his election on such ground that he cannot possibly save it afterwards.*

Military victories before the November 8 election were a major factor in the Union party victory. Admiral David Farragut, of "Damn the torpedoes" fame, closed Mobile Bay, the last gulf port left to the Confederacy, on September 2. General William T. Sherman captured Atlanta on September 2, and General Philip Sheridan's troops were victorious at Winchester, Virginia, on September 19. The North was jubilant over Sherman's and Sheridan's victories, and supporters of Lincoln grew in numbers while critical voices were muted.

Every effort was made to allow Union soldiers to vote, for the service vote was thought to be critical in Pennsylvania and Ohio. Both parties were supported by organizations formed by veterans. The veteran Union Club supported Lincoln, while the Democrats had the "McClellan Legion." Both organizations paraded, demonstrated, and held mass meetings. Eleven of the northern states made it possible for their soldiers to vote at the front. After the October elections in Pennsylvania, Ohio, and Indiana showed gains for the Union ticket, *Harper's Weekly* reported that "unless all human foresight fails, the election of Abraham Lincoln and Andrew Johnson is assured."

Lincoln received 2,213,665 popular votes, McClellan 1,802,237.

Although McClellan received 45 percent of the popular vote, he carried only three states: Delaware, New Jersey, and Kentucky. Lincoln received 212 votes in the Electoral College, McClellan 21.

THE PLATFORMS.

BALTIMORE.

The National Convention which assembled at Baltimore on the 7th of last June, and there nominated ABRAHAM LINCOLN for re-election as President, with ANDREW JOHNSON as Vice-President, adopted and presented to the American People the following

PLATFORM.

Resolved, That it is the highest duty of every American citizen to maintain against all their enemies the integrity of the Union, and the paramount authority of the Constitution and laws of the United States; and that, laying aside all differences of political opinion, we pledge ourselves as Union men, animated by a common sentiment, and aiming at a common object, to do everything in our power to aid the Government in quelling by force of arms the rebellion now raging against its authority, and in bringing to the punishment due to their crimes the rebels and traitors arrayed against it.

Resolved, That we approve the determination of the Government of the United States not to compromise with rebels, nor to offer any terms of peace except such as may be based upon an "unconditional surrender" of their hostility and a return to their just allegiance to the Constitution and laws of the United States, and that we call upon the Government to maintain this position and to prosecute the war with the utmost possible vigor to the complete suppression of the Rebellion, in full reliance upon the self-sacrifice, the patriotism, the heroic valor, and the undying devotion of the American people to their country and its free institutions.

Resolved, That, as Slavery was the cause, and now constitutes the strength, of this rebellion, and as it must be always and everywhere hostile to the principles of republican government, justice and the national safety demand its utter and complete extirpation from the soil of the republic; and that we uphold and maintain the acts and proclamations by which the Government, in its own defense, has aimed a death-blow at this gigantic evil. We are in favor, furthermore, of such an amendment to the Constitution, to be made by the people in conformity with its provisions, as shall terminate and forever prohibit the existence of Slavery within the limits of the jurisdiction of the United States.

Resolved, That the thanks of the American People are due to the soldiers and sailors of the Army and Navy, who have periled their lives in defense of their country, and in vindication of the honor of the flag; that the nation owes to them some permanent recognition of their patriotism and valor, and ample and permanent provision for those of their survivors who have received disabling and honorable wounds in the service of the country; and that the memories of those who have fallen in its defense shall be held in grateful and everlasting remembrance.

Resolved, That we approve and applaud the practical wisdom, the unselfish patriotism, and unswerving fidelity to the Constitution and the principles of American liberty, with which Abraham Lincoln has discharged, under circumstances of unparalleled difficulty, the great duties and responsibilities of the Presidential office; that we approve and indorse, as demanded by the emergency and essential to the preservation of the nation, and as within the Constitution, the measures and acts which he has adopted to defend the nation against its open and secret foes; that we approve especially the Proclamation of Emancipation, and the employment as Union soldiers of men heretofore held in Slavery; and that we have full confidence in his determination to carry these and all other constitutional measures essential to the salvation of the country into full and complete effect.

Resolved, That we deem it essential to the general welfare that harmony should prevail in the National councils, and we regard as worthy of public confidence and official trust those only who cordially indorse the principles proclaimed in these resolutions, and which should characterize the administration of the Government.

Resolved, That the Government owes to all men employed in its armies, without regard to distinction of color, the full protection of the laws of war; and that any violation of these laws or of the usages of civilized nations in the time of war by the Rebels now in arms, should be made the subject of full and prompt redress.

Resolved, That the foreign immigration, which in the past has added so much to the wealth and development of resources and increase of power to this nation, the asylum of the oppressed of all nations, should be fostered and encouraged by a liberal and just policy.

Resolved, That we are in favor of the speedy construction of a Railroad to the Pacific.

Resolved, That the National faith, pledged for the redemption of the Public Debt, must be kept inviolate; and that for this purpose we recommend economy and rigid responsibility in the public expenditures, and a vigorous and just system of taxation; that it is the duty of every loyal State to sustain the credit and promote the use of the National Currency.

Resolved, That we approve the position taken by the Government that the people of the United States never regarded with indifference the attempt of any European power to overthrow by force, or to supplant by fraud, the institutions of any republican government on the western continent, and that they view with extreme jealousy, as menacing to the peace and independence of this our country, the efforts of any such power to obtain new footholds for monarchical governments, sustained by a foreign military force, in near proximity to the United States.

CHICAGO.

The Democratic National Convention which gathered at Chicago on the 29th of August, and presented the names of GEORGE B. McCLELLAN for President, and GEORGE H. PENDLETON for Vice-President, agreed on and adopted the following

PLATFORM.

Resolved, That in the future, as in the past, we will adhere with unswerving fidelity to the Union under the Constitution, as the only solid foundation of our strength, security, and happiness as a people, and as a frame-work of goverment equally conducive to the welfare and prosperity of all the States, both Northern and Southern.

Resolved, That this Convention does explicitly declare, as the sense of the American People, that, after four years of failure to restore the Union by the experiment of war, during which, under the pretense of a military necessity of a war power higher than the Constitution, the Constitution itself has been disregarded in every part, and public liberty and private right alike trodden down, and the material prosperity of the country essentially impaired, justice, humanity, liberty, and the public welfare, demand that immediate efforts be made for a cessation of hostilities, with a view to an ultimate Convention of all the States, or other peaceable means to the end that at the earliest practicable moment peace may be restored on the basis of the Federal Union of the States.

Resolved, That the direct interference of the military authority of the United States in the recent elections held in Kentucky, Maryland, Missouri and Delaware, was a shameful violation of the Constitution, and the repetition of such acts in the approaching election will be held as revolutionary, and resisted with all the means and power under our control.

Resolved, That the aim and object of the Democratic party is to preserve the Federal Union and the rights of the States unimpaired; and they hereby declare that they consider the Administrative usurpation of extraordinary and dangerous powers not granted by the Constitution, the subversion of the civil by military law in States not in insurrection, the arbitrary military arrest, imprisonment, trial and sentence of American citizens in States where civil law exists in full force, the suppression of freedom of speech and of the press, the denial of the right of asylum, the open and avowed disregard of State rights, the employment of unusual test-oaths, and the interference with and denial of the right of the people to bear arms, as calculated to prevent a restoration of the Union and the perpetuation of a government deriving its just powers from the consent of the governed.

Resolved, That the shameful disregard of the Administration to its duty in respect to our fellow citizens who now and long have been prisoners of war in a suffering condition, deserves the severest reprobation, on the score alike of public interest and common humanity.

Resolved, That the sympathy of the Democratic party is heartily and earnestly extended to the soldiery of our army, who are and have been in the field under the flag of our country; and, in the event of our attaining power, they will receive all the care and protection, regard and kindness, that the brave soldiers of the Republic have so nobly earned.

POINTS OF DIFFERENCE.

The rival Platforms just given, differ, as will be seen, mainly on these points:

1. The Union Platform affirms that the Union is to be *maintained* " by quelling by force of arms the Rebellion now raging against its authority;" while the Democratic Platform condemns the National effort to do this as a failure, and demands "immediate efforts for a cessation of hostilities" with a view to "peace at the earliest practicable moment." In other words: The Union Platform looks to the ending of the war through the defeat and overthrow of the Rebellion, while the Democratic contemplates peace through the virtual triumph of the traitors.

2. The Union Platform regards Slavery as the inciting, guilty cause of the Rebellion, and demands the suppression of that cause in the interest of "justice and the National safety." The Democratic is silent in terms as to Slavery, but manifestly contemplates its perpetuation and fortification under the "restored" Union it longs for.

3. The Union Platform regards the Rebellion as flagrantly *wrong*—iniquitous, inexcusable, and justly exposing its contrivers to punishment. The Democratic, on the other hand, has no word of condemnation for the treason, nor of reproof for its authors.

4. The Union Platform approves generally and heartily the efforts of President Lincoln and his Cabinet to put down the Rebels and save the Republic. The Democratic, on the other hand, condemns the official action of the President and his Cabinet most sweepingly; finding fault with their almost every act as arbitrary, usurping and pernicious.

5. While the Democratic Platform proffers sympathy to the soldiers and sailors fighting against the Rebels, it nowhere intimates that the cause for which they fight is righteous and just. It censures our own Government for the cruelties and privations which our captured soldiers have endured at the hands of the Rebels, but has no word of condemnation for their authors. The Union Platform not only returns the thanks of the American People to our soldiers and sailors, but proposes a National recognition of their patriotism and valor, with permanent provision for those disabled in their country's service, and efficient protection for so many as are exposed to peculiar perils.

Freemen of the United States! read, mark, weigh, resolve, and VOTE!

This is preëminently a contest regarding important principles and measures, compared with which, personal considerations are of small account.

For sale by all News Agents. Price, $1 per 100.

156. The Democratic candidate for president in 1864, George Brinton McClellan, shown here with his wife, Ellen Mary Marcy McClellan, was a controversial Union general in the Civil War. He was, according to many of his contemporaries, excellent in training and organizing his troops but cautious in engaging the enemy. He had a penchant for overestimating Confederate strength and always demanded more of everything. Vain, opinionated, but loved by his troops, he referred to Lincoln as the "original gorilla" and was pleased to be known as the "young Napoleon." After the Battle of Antietam, when a quick follow-up might have destroyed General Robert E. Lee's army, McClellan failed to take advantage of the situation and was relieved of his command, never again to be employed in the field.

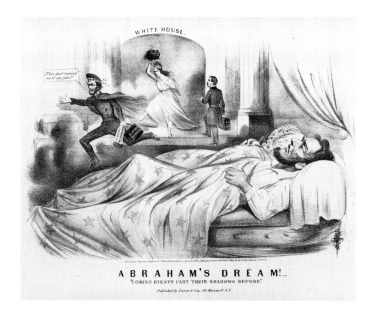

157. In *Abraham's Dream!,* a black-and-white Currier & Ives lithographed cartoon published in October 1864, just before the November presidential election, Columbia, under the archway of the White House, brandishes the severed head of a black man at the fleeing Lincoln who grumbles, "This don't remind me of any joke!!" Lincoln carries a scroll labeled "To whom it may concern" and a handbag marked "A. Lincoln Illinois." The Scotsman's hat he is wearing, a fictitious headgear invented by a journalist, is to remind viewers of Lincoln's secret ride through Baltimore on his inaugural journey to Washington in 1861. The Democratic candidate, General McClellan, is shown about to enter the White House.

158. *Running the "Machine,"* a Currier & Ives black-and-white election poster, was published in 1864 prior to the presidential election. The new secretary of the treasury, William Pitt Fessenden (Salmon Chase had resigned from the post on June 29), turns a machine producing greenbacks for greedy contractors. Secretary of War Edwin Stanton receives a message of a minor Union victory and wants General John A. Dix to be notified. Lincoln prepares to tell a joke. William H. Seward, secretary of state, wants revenge on someone who called him "A. Humbug." Secretary of the Navy Gideon Welles (whose name is misspelled) shows his ignorance of naval affairs.

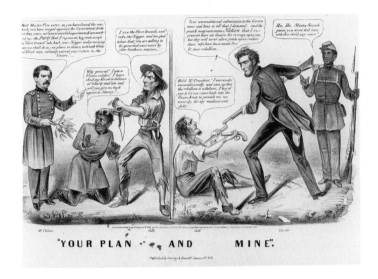

"YOUR PLAN — AND MINE".

A LITTLE GAME OF BAGATELLE, BETWEEN OLD ABE THE RAIL SPLITTER & LITTLE MAC THE GUNBOAT GENERAL.

159. This two-paneled black-and-white lithographed cartoon, *Your Plan and Mine,* was published by Currier & Ives in October 1864. At left, McClellan offers an olive branch to Jefferson Davis, implying that if elected he would permit the slave states to reenter the Union with slavery intact. At right, Lincoln tells "Jeff," who is surrendering his weapons, that Lincoln's reelection would mean the end of slavery, but that the Union would take no revenge upon the Confederate states in permitting them to reenter the Union.

160. *A Little Game of Bagatelle* was published by J. L. Magee in Philadelphia during the campaign of 1864. The cartoon shows the two presidential candidates, McClellan and Lincoln, with their respective running mates, as well as General Ulysses S. Grant, who took no part in the campaign. Seated on the right is Clement Laird Vallandigham, an Ohio politician who led the peace Democrats, or "copperheads." He opposed Lincoln and the Civil War and was arrested and imprisoned for what was held to be treasonous activity. Banished to the South, he subsequently took up residence in Canada. He returned illegally to Ohio in 1864, attended the Democratic Convention in Chicago and forced approval of the plank in the Democratic platform that called the war a failure and demanded cessation of military action. McClellan, the Democratic nominee, repudiated this plank.

THE TRUE ISSUE OR "THATS WHATS THE MATTER".

THE "RAIL SPLITTER" AT WORK REPAIRING THE UNION.

161. In this black-and-white lithographed cartoon published by Currier & Ives shortly after McClellan was nominated on August 31, 1864, the general ignores the peace platform of his Democratic party and campaigns for continuation of the war as the best way: "The Union must be preserved at all hazards!" Lincoln says, "No peace without Abolition!" and Davis, "No peace without Separation!"

162. Andrew Johnson, Lincoln's 1864 running mate and a former tailor, is shown stitching the Union together with the aid of Lincoln, who holds the globe steady with a rail. The artist, J. E. Baken, has signed his name, but the lithographed cartoon bears no imprint of a publisher.

Second Presidential Campaign; Second Administration 77

THE OLD BULL DOG ON THE RIGHT TRACK.

163. *Slow & Steady Wins the Race*, published during the presidential campaign of 1864, demonstrates the contradiction between the Democratic platform and the party nominee. Candidate McClellan rides two animals: the war-horse "Brag & Bluster," indicative of his desire to save the Union, and the donkey "Fawn & Cringe," which represents the peace platform he tried to repudiate. Lincoln, riding the Union roadster "Slow and Steady," leads the race. "The Ohio Clown" is Clement Laird Vallandigham, the Democrat who forced the peace plank into the party platform. The artist and publisher of this lithographed cartoon are unknown.

164. The bulldog, General Grant, sits astride the Petersburg and Weldon Railroad, the supply route to the Confederate capital of Richmond. Jefferson Davis sits in the doghouse, with General Lee to the left and P. G. T. Beauregard to the right. McClellan pleads with Lincoln to call Grant off before he hurts someone. Lincoln reminds McClellan that "thats the same pack of curs, that chased you aboard of the Gunboat two years ago." Grant stands ready to pounce on Richmond: "I'm bound to take it." This black-and-white cartoon was published by Currier & Ives for the presidential campaign of 1864.

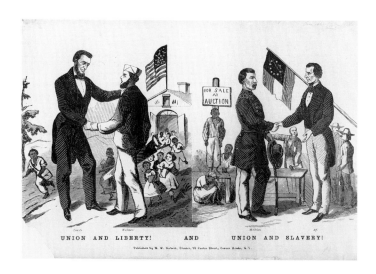

UNION AND LIBERTY! AND UNION AND SLAVERY!

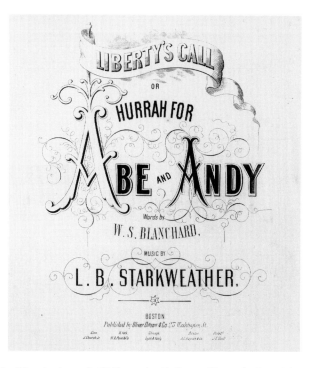

165. M. W. Siebert of New York published this two-paneled lithographed cartoon, which shows the voter's choices in 1864. A vote for Lincoln, shown here shaking hands with a workman, will bring "Union and Liberty!" A vote for McClellan, shown shaking hands with Jefferson Davis, will save the Union but will not abolish slavery.

166. The lyrics of "Liberty's Call or Hurrah for Abe and Andy," sheet music that circulated during the presidential race of 1864, urge voters to back the Union candidates.

> *Freeman rouse in strength divine*
> *And shout for Abe and Andy,*
> *Bright the stars of freedom shine,*
> *Hurrah for Abe and Andy!*
> *In serried rank, triumphant host,*
> *Freeman onward to your post,*
> *Let proud Columbia be your boast,*
> *Hurrah for Abe and Andy!*

W. S. Blanchard wrote the lyrics, and L. B. Starkweather the music. Oliver Ditson of Boston published the song.

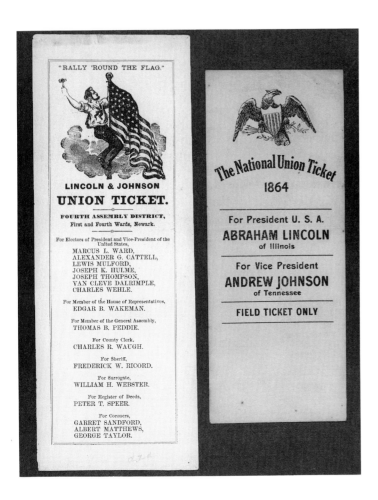

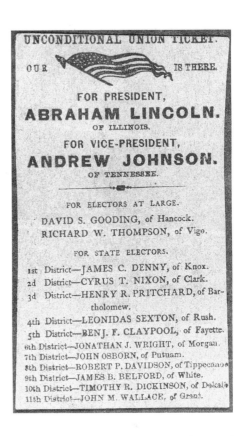

167. Handbills list the Union (Republican) party ticket for the 1864 election. At left is the ticket for the Fourth Assembly District, First and Fourth Wards, Newark, New Jersey. The one on the right is not identified as to location.

169. This small broadside (shown original size, 2⅜ by 4 inches) lists the 1864 "Unconditional Union Ticket" for Indiana. On its reverse side are the words "Greenbacks, Greenbacks," and the paper is green, probably to resemble the paper currency then in circulation. Electors and their home counties are listed for the eleven congressional districts, as well as two electors at large.

168. The 1864 Union party tickets for Illinois, Indiana, and Ohio. On the reverse of the Indiana ticket, center, printed in large letters, is a plea, "Stand by the President! Rally Once Again!" The reverse of the Ohio ticket has a cut of the American eagle and the admonition "Rally 'round the Flag, Boys! Rally once again!"

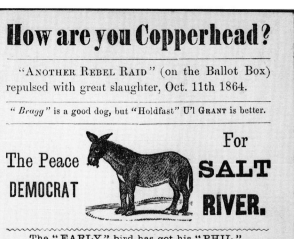

How are you Copperhead?

"ANOTHER REBEL RAID" (on the Ballot Box)
repulsed with great slaughter, Oct. 11th 1864.

"*Bragg*" is a good dog, but "Holdfast" U'l GRANT is better.

The Peace DEMOCRAT / For SALT RIVER.

The "EARLY" bird has got his "PHIL,"
And Loyalty's triumphant still.

"HONEST ABE" will furnish another **G**un **B**oat
for "Little Mac" in November.

170. This small card (shown original size, 3⅛ by 3 inches) mocking the Democrats probably was reproduced in Ohio. There, as well as in Indiana and Pennsylvania, the Union party made gains in the October 1864 congressional elections. Ohio was the home of Clement L. Vallandigham, the peace Democrat, better known as a "copperhead." The statement "'Bragg' is a good dog, but 'Holdfast' U'l Grant is better" refers to Confederate General Braxton Bragg, who planned the defense of Richmond, which Grant was assaulting. "The 'Early' bird has got his 'Phil'" refers to Confederate General Jubal Anderson Early, who was outgeneraled by Philip (Little Phil) Henry Sheridan in the Shenandoah Valley campaign beginning in August 1864. The last sentence, referring to "another Gun Boat for 'Little Mac,'" is to remind readers of the abortive peninsular campaign proposed by General McClellan in 1862.

171. The four-page newspaper *Father Abraham*, supporting Lincoln for a second term, was published in Reading, Pennsylvania, by E. H. Rauch and his son, W. H. Rauch. In this first number, published on August 1, 1864, the editor announced that it would be published every Tuesday morning until after the election.

172. This forty-six-page booklet, *The Lincoln Catechism*, contains a vicious tirade against Lincoln and his supporters. J. F. Feeks, a New York publisher, furnished copies of his many publications to Democratic clubs at a reduced rate. The first lesson in the catechism goes like this:

What is the Constitution?
A compact with hell—now obsolete.
By whom hath the Constitution been made obsolete?
By Abraham Africanus the First.
To what end?
That his days may be long in office—and that he make himself and his people the equal of the negroes.
What is a President?
A general agent for negroes.

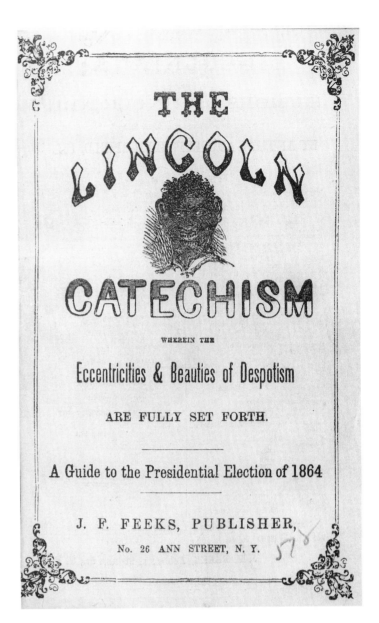

PLATFORMS ILLUSTRATED

173. *Platforms Illustrated* is a Union-party-inspired two-paneled lithographed cartoon that circulated during the campaign of 1864. At left, Lincoln, blessed by Miss Liberty ("My fate I trust in your hands, go and do your Duty!"), sits on a card-table platform supported by Senator Charles Sumner of Massachusetts, General Grant, and Admiral Farragut. At right, Clement L. Vallandigham, the peace Democrat, lifts General McClellan onto a head of cheese that is being attacked by copperheads. The *London Times* is represented as supporting McClellan. Also shown are Horatio Seymour, governor of New York, who presided at the 1864 Democratic convention in Chicago, and Fernando Wood, mayor of New York, who was a leader of the peace Democrats. The lithograph contains no publisher's imprint or copyright entry.

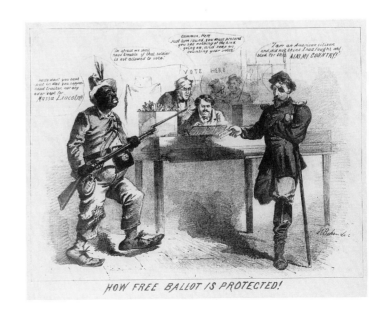

HOW FREE BALLOT IS PROTECTED!

174. This lithographed cartoon graphically accuses the Union party of stuffing the ballot box in the 1864 election. It is signed by the artist, J. E. Baken, but does not contain a publisher's imprint.

PUBLISHED BY CURRIER & IVES.   Entered according to Act of Congress, in the year 1864, by Currier & Ives, in the Clerk's Office of the District Court of the United States, for the Southern District of New York.   152 NASSAU St NEW YORK.

GRAND BANNER OF THE RADICAL DEMOCRACY,
FOR 1864.

175. *Grand Banner of the Radical Democracy*, a hand-colored Currier & Ives lithograph of 1864 featuring General John C. Frémont and General John Cochrane, portrays a minor rift in Union party ranks in 1864. Toward the end of May, a few dissenting Republicans, German-Americans, and war Democrats met in Cleveland and nominated Frémont for president and Cochrane as his running mate. When no great groundswell arose for the nominees, both withdrew on September 11. One day later, Postmaster General Montgomery Blair resigned from Lincoln's Cabinet. Some historians contend that a deal had been cut: Frémont would take himself out of the campaign if Lincoln would discharge Blair, Frémont's bitter enemy.

PEACE & DISUNION!

WHAT IS MEANT BY AN
IMMEDIATE CESSATION OF HOSTILITIES?

It means the withdrawal of our Armies from Louisiana, Mississippi, Arkansas, Alabama, Florida, Georgia, Tennessee, North Carolina, South Carolina and Virginia. It means the raising of the Blockade. It means allowing the Rebels to supply themselves with men and money, and munitions of war. It means the abandonment of all that we have gained; the acknowledgment that the war is a failure, that we are defeated, and that we cannot subdue the rebellion. In short, it means the

DISMEMBERMENT OF THE UNION!

WHAT IS MEANT BY A
CONVENTION OF THE STATES?

It means that we shall beg the South to grant us a treaty of peace, the first condition of which they have proclaimed to be the recognition of their independence. It means that we shall surrender to them half the territory of the Union, and hold the rest on such terms as they shall dictate.

WHAT IS MEANT BY A
SEPARATION OF THE UNION?

It means two or more military nations involved in perpetual war with each other. It means the destruction of our industry and the loss of our liberties. It means huge standing armies recruited by incessant drafts. It means the burden of unlimited expenditure without resources or credit to defray it. It means yearly invasions and desolation. It means anarchy and desolation.

Citizens, reflect that this is what you vote for if you vote

THE DEMOCRATIC TICKET.

King & Baird, Printers, 607 Sansom Street, Philad'a

IS IT PEACE OR WAR?

THE CHICAGO PLATFORM.

" *Resolved*, That this Convention does explicitly declare, as the sense of the American people, that after four years of failure to restore the Union by the experiment of war, justice, humanity, liberty, and the public welfare demand that immediate efforts be made for a cessation of hostilities, with a view to an ultimate Convention of all the States, or other peaceable means, to the end that at the earliest practicable moment peace may be restored on the basis of the Federal Union."

The Chicago Candidates.

McCLELLAN.

"**Such a rebellion cannot be justified** upon ethical grounds, and the only alternatives for our choice are its suppression, or the destruction of our nationality. . . . Shall it be said in after ages that we lacked the vigor to complete the work thus begun? That after all these noble lives freely given, we hesitated and failed to keep straight on till our land was saved."
WEST POINT ORATION, June 15th, 1864.

" I could not look in the face of my gallant comrades of the Army and Navy, who have fought in so many bloody battles, and tell them that their labors and the sacrifice of so many of our slain and wounded brethren had been in vain."
LETTER OF ACCEPTANCE, Sept. 8th, 1864.

PENDLETON.

" Now, sir, what force of arms can compel a State to do what she has agreed to do? What force of arms can compel a State to refrain from doing that which her State Government, supported by the sentiment of her people, is determined to persist in doing? . . . Sir, the whole scheme of coercion is impracticable. It is contrary to the genius and spirit of the Constitution.

. . . Let the seceding States depart in peace; let them establish their government and empire, and work out their destiny according to the wisdom which God has given them."
SPEECH IN CONGRESS, Jan. 18th, 1861.

DEMOCRATS can you tell whether you are asked to vote for

PEACE OR WAR, UNION OR DISUNION?

King & Baird, Printers, 607 Sansom Street, Philadelphia.

176. The Union League of Philadelphia published this 1864 broadside, measuring 18½ by 12½ inches, in an effort to confuse the Democrats. The league, as the name makes obvious, was a vocal supporter of the Union. Military reverses in 1862 had led to low morale among many citizens in the North. To help counteract it, a booster organization called the Union League formed in Pekin, Illinois, in June 1862. The movement spread throughout the North, and by mid-1863 a national headquarters had been established in Washington. The league sponsored parades and speeches at mass meetings and distributed tons of printed matter supporting the Union party ticket of Lincoln and Johnson.

177. This broadside, measuring 18½ by 23½ inches, is a companion to the preceding "Peace & Disunion!" It seeks to frighten potential Democratic voters. It too was published by the Union League of Philadelphia.

National Union League Gazette.

NO. 1. PHILADELPHIA, OCTOBER, 1864. VOL. I.

The Torchlight of Liberty in Full Flame.

TREMENDOUS DEMONSTRATION AT THE NATIONAL UNION LEAGUE HALL.

GEN. JOHN COCHRANE, OF NEW YORK, Delivers a Thrilling Speech.

Gen. SIMON CAMERON, Makes a Few Introductory Remarks.

Saturday evening 1st inst., will long be remembered by the lovers of the Union, who were fortunate enough to gain admittance into the spacious Union League Hall. The many thousands in the State who could not be present, will be refreshed, and re-inspirited, and patriotically enlightened by the following gems:

At the appointed hour General Cochrane, flanked right and left by General Cameron and Morton McMichael, Esq., was conducted to the rostrum, accompanied by a delegation from the National Union League. The audience arose and cheered enthusiastically, the band playing the "Star Spangled Banner."

The applause having subsided, Morton McMichael, Esq., arose and briefly said that the people had assembled to night to listen to a gentleman who had done active service on the battle field of the nation, to testify his veneration for the National Government and the deep interest he feels in the contest now pending. [Applause.] Before he speaks, General Cameron, Chairman of the State Executive Committee, will make a few remarks [Great applause.]

GENERAL CAMERON'S REMARKS.

The venerable Chairman of the Union Executive Committee of the State, General Cameron, being thus introduced, said that he had come to the meeting to-night to introduce General John Cochrane, of New York. [Applause.] It gave the speaker infinite pleasure to say that he had known him for years as a public man, and of all public men he knew of no one actuated by more solid or disinterested patriotism than he. [Great applause.]

It so happened that in the early period of the rebellion he, the speaker, had something to do, because of an official position that he then held. He had his own views, the same as any other man. At that time General Cochrane, then a Democrat, called upon him and offered his services to assist in crushing the rebellion. He speedily raised a regiment, and in a short time was ready on the field. Hundreds and thousands of men offered—there was an uprising throughout the land. It may be said that the country was overrun with patriots ready and anxious to resent the insult given to the flag of the Union. [Applause.]

General Cochrane's views and my own agreed as to the method of squelching the rebellion. A *carte blanche* was given him, and in a short time he responded with twelve or thirteen hundred men. Gen. Cochrane, in that time of excitement, calmly viewed the contending elements, and in progressing with the war he made certain suggestions, or propositions, that have since proved true, and are now established as the policy of the Government.—[Rounds of applause.]

General Cochrane, then in the field, thought that arms ought to be placed in the hands of everybody who panted for an opportunity to defend the Union, and put down the rebels at once. [Applause.] The speaker agreed with him, and in the endeavor to effect so desirable an object, papers denounced him; but history now records the same views as the policy of the Government. It is the true policy. There are now in the field two hundred thousand Americans of African descent. [Applause.] These men have at least saved to the country two hundred thousand white men. [Renewed applause.] We agreed then, as we do now, that every one who bore arms in defence of the country, who risked his life, or shed his blood, should no longer be a slave. [Tremendous applause.] No man will doubt that this is the true policy of the country now. [Applause.] As for slavery itself, that will be settled by the progress of the war. [More applause.] General Cameron now proceeded to show the great importance of standing shoulder to shoulder in this contest; with a full reliance upon Divine Providence, urge by all honorable means the re-election of President Lincoln. [Long continued applause.] The country at this time can get no other man to do better than Abraham Lincoln. [Applause.] As the war progresses we are the better enabled to speak from experience, and he was free to say that the President is too sagacious not to take notice of the signs of the times; he felt free to say that when he is re-elected he will call around him a new set of men, who will give him the required support, and bring the rebellion to a speedy close, and a lasting, honorable peace. [Tremendous and long continued applause.] New men who will cheerfully assist him.—[Renewed applause.] This is the feeling in the State, and with this feeling we renew our efforts, and that he will be triumphantly elected there can not be a single doubt among intelligent men. [Great applause.] Gen. Cameron now alluded to a tour that he had just taken in parts of the State, and he assured the immense audience that, in all his experience as a public man, he never saw such enthusiasm; the fires of patriotism are burning brightly on the mountain and in the vale; the old flag floats in the pure gushing breeze of the interior, cheering the heart of every patriot, and making him feel anxious for the day to come when he shall cast a full vote to sustain that glorious emblem of our nationality by supporting all its standard bearers. We shall have increased strength in the Legislature. [Applause.] We shall have a fuller representation in Congress. [More applause.] Remember that there never was a time that the November election did not increase the vote over that polled in October; then let us prepare for the State contest, carry our ticket, and the vote for President Lincoln and Johnson in the following month will be so overwhelming as to break down the already crushed spirit of the rebellion and its leaders. [Enthusiastic applause] General Cameron now very handsomely introduced General John Cochrane, amid the wildest applause from every part of the room.

SPEECH OF GENERAL COCHRANE, OF NEW YORK.

My experience, fellow Union men of Philadelphia, has always taught me that in the great army of freedom the trouble has generally been at the rear; never at the front (in allusion to a slight disorder prevailing at the end of the hall). I am happy that the little occurrence of this evening has affirmed that lesson, and that I have the assurance, before I shall undertake to deliver a few opinions I have to present to you, that I stand here to-night, where I have always been desirous of standing when my country was in peril, among its friends, its champions, and its supporters. [Applause.] Man's efforts are feeble and of little worth. When the elemental war rages, and havoc is the order of events, human efforts must be subservient to the order of affairs; but woe, woe to those who lift their puny arms against the decrees of Providence, and assert humanity against Omnipotence. We are in that position. The national elements are at war. Peace flies shrieking from the field. Bloody hands of warlike antagonists grasp each other fiercely, and the shock is for national life. Shall your country live or die? On and towards that question are arrayed forces above and beyond ours. We can but look with awe and reverence at the swelling sea. We can but bow our heads with all humility beneath the fiery ordeal and still proclaim that what lies in us we will accomplish. What there is for patriotism to do we will effectuate; and in no event, within the pale at least of this sanctuary, here in Philadelphia, of American Independence, shall the traitor's arm be lifted unpunished, or the traitor's front be raised unrebuked. [Applause.] I can but be obliged to my friend (for I am proud to be permitted to term him friend) for this unmerited and undeserved compliment.

There was no merit in what he so tersely repeated; but had those efforts been impeded there had been great shame. I am not alone. I stand with an army of my fellow-citizens around me. Look upon yonder halting soldier! Look upon yonder lame and stricken officer. Hear those groans and lamentations, and above all listen to the sweet notes of that patriot song that from children, mothers, brothers' lips issues in glorious harmony and keeps tune to "the music of the Union." [Applause.] There, oh Americans, are your soldiers! They stand for you in yonder field. They bare their bosoms to the rude shock of war that you may be saved, and never, no never, at any period has that patriot throng tired, but always with steady tramp and iron nerve advanced against the foe, exclaiming with every cadenced step, "Down with your arms, rebels!" [Applause.] Down with your arms, rebels, is all that loyal soldiers ask of their rebellious brothers. And when their arms shall be grounded, as full sure they will be; when your ensigns shall float over yon statue of the Father of his Country in the State House of Richmond; when throughout this whole land the glorious shout of freemen shall be as harmonious as it was when erst here, in your Independence Hall, it rang throughout a united nation—then, oh then, it will be the glad shout will here again arise and move in every direction, over hill and dell. That shall be the noblest meed and the bravest reward for those soldiers in arms who have effected your safety, re-established our nationality, and driven back rebellion whence it came. [Applause.] I do not intend to detain you here long, fellow-citizens, this evening. I have come to make a few initiatory remarks preliminary to a short and transient career among you in discussing a political debate upon which hangs as much the peace of your country as hangs the contests in the field. Let us advance Richmondward to-night, and let Pennsylvania pronounce for a traitorous peace to-morrow, and farewell to the hopes of this country. [Applause.] The battle field of freedom now is expanding before us. Here in your streets and at your hearths there are to be found the altars of freedom. Sacrifice these with a penitence that shall never be negligent. Sacrifice all political prejudice, and turning in your footsteps encourage those patriot soldiers who are now looking as anxiously and longingly towards that stronghold of treason. Richmond, as towards Philadelphia, the altar of liberty and American Independence. [Applause.]

It has occurred to me, therefore, to detain you but a short while with a running commentary upon the position to which we have attained; not the material position of war merely, the position which principle requires that you should establish and decide. Without this principle you are at loss, floating and buffeted upon a tempestuous ocean. What is the issue? As I have been taught to believe, party issues are buried, obliterated, effaced. Ask yourselves what issue is there now prevailing that once decided and discriminated between what was formerly a Republican and Democratic party. None. Both claim to be Union lovers; both claim to be Union preservers. The great issue upon which we stand divided had never been dreampt of, certainly had never protruded out above the barrier of party politics. Suddenly the detonation of arms was heard; suddenly the explosion of war stunned your ears. The din of marching myriads was heard over the land, and now, after nearly four years of conflict, we stand here this night with that identical issue thus created, and thus prepared for you to accept, discuss, determine. What is the issue? My fellow citizens, is it not singular that here upon the eve of a great election circumstances should warrant the propounding of such a question?—and is it not very singular that however plain and transparent events may be, there are those among us who are altogether bewildered, if not entirely benighted, upon one subject which constitutes the force and efficacy of this occasion? Why, the issue is plainly and definitely Union on the one side and disunion on the other. [Applause.] Precipitated, as I have already declared to you to war, the inquiry arises, how was the issue prepared? Why, I am answered here and there throughout this vast throng, that the main preparation has been from the foundation of our Government; from the period of its recognition of the institution of slavery. This, fellow-citizens, in many respects is true; but it requires some discussion in order to present properly the bearing and true import of the proposition upon the theory of which moves this war. I, for one, believe this: That the simple issue of Union and disunion is the issue as between superior and inferior civilization. It is, in truth, a war between incompatible forces. Now do not be alarmed with the imagination that I am to engage in and present to you an abstruce argument here this evening. Nothing is farther from my intention; but I may say to this: That from the moment within the bosom of one constituted government two systems of labor were introduced—namely, slave labor at the South and paid labor at the North—two incompatible and explosive elements were permitted to enter that ultimately must have produced the very war in which we are engaged. [Applause.] It is immaterial whether the immediate cause of this war was that your fiery Southerner was not gratified with the protection of slavery in the Territories, nor is it of any moment whatever that he had or had not all the constitutional guarantees that he claimed. It is of consequence, however, for me and all of you to determine that the cause which has effected this divergence of the two sections of the country and ultimately produced conflict, was a cause located far back in our history, dating from the very moment when our Government was established partly with slave labor and partly with free labor. Then, fellow-citizens, if this divergence has been in the order of events, there could have been no possibility of a parallel continuation of these forces within the same Government. Can you be surprised that at any continuous period of the history of that Government, a war identical with the war upon us should have been precipitated? Then if you will but associate my previous remarks with my present, you will immediately perceive that that which now is represented by the Union on one side, was then at the commencement of our Government up to the present represented as the Union principle, namely, the free laboring classes of the North. And that which represented disunion was the other element of slave labor, or, "the peculiar institution." Apply, then, this reasoning to the present events, and you have in the field—what?—Two contending armies—one for the Union, the other for disunion. Then at the North, as at the South, the one sole issue, as it has always been where these two forces come in collision with each other, is Union or disunion. [Applause.] Now, fellow citizens, let me for a moment or two examine the attitude of the question as it rests at the front, as it is accepted by the soldier in the ranks, as it is pointed by the bayonet in the field. Let me see; General Lee orders his cohorts to advance. They do advance. A fierce and bloody conflict is begun. Down goes the patriot, his rebel brother interlocked in the grasp of death. The shout, the shriek, the wretched contortion, and the glorious cry of triumph, all blend together—for what? Is it for a little better Union? Is it for a little less Union? Is it for Union with a little slavery on one side, or is it Union on the other with not quite so much slavery? No! It is on the one side, the Union; and on the other, for disunion. [Applause.] There is no palaver in the ranks about the Union as it was, but every musket that explodes enunciates the doctrine very articulately, the Union as it should be. [Applause.] You may listen to the detonation of the heavy guns on the Southern side a whole summer's day, and you will never hear pronounced, nor can that fearful commentary be forced into any other construction than recognition of Southern independence. What! Hood flying from Atlanta! What! Early flying down the Valley? What? Lee retiring into Richmond! [applause] and all that they may come back into the Union? Sheridan in hot pursuit. [Applause.] Sherman, with his invincible courage and ample resources, driving the rebel dogs before him. [Applause.] Grant—[applause]—Unconditional Surrender Grant—has his hold upon the throat of the rebellion, with no commentary, with no discussion, but with the sword's point, clarifying and rectifying, in one simple, sharp, decisive phrase, the Union, the Union, the Union forever. [Applause.] That is the logic of war; and who talks of chopping logic, or ingenious dialectics, or logical sequences, when the cannon's mouth is proclaiming war? No, simple and clear, pure and intelligible as is the English language, is the attitude of that army at the front. Lay down your arms and you shall have such a Union as we choose to give you. [Applause.] Why talk they of rights, who have shed our brothers' blood without provocation. Rights! They have the constitutional rights which we may confer upon them, but not under the Constitution which they themselves have trampled in the mire. [Applause.] Rights they have, and rights they shall have, the common rights claimed and required by all humanity.

[At this juncture a large number of the First Battalion Union Campaign Club, returned veterans, under the command of Col. Ellmaker, entered the hall, when much enthusiasm followed.]

The speaker continued: I had arrived at a point where the opportune arrival of reinforcements interrupted me. [Applause.] I had succeeded, I trust, in making myself understood upon the one important point of how essential to us was the action in the field of our armies in settling the one issue of Union or disunion in which we are all engaged. I had stated to you the process of that settlement, and indicated on the one side the armies of the North, and on the other the army of rebellion. Let us see how stands that issue, and how early we may expect its decision. These armies have now been engaged nearly four years. The old Army of the Potomac, the worthy and renowned representative of

178. The Union League of Philadelphia published this one-page paper, the *National Union League Gazette,* in October 1864, supporting Lincoln for a second term in the White House. Seven numbers of the paper were published, and they contained speeches of prominent Republicans, letters from Union officers, and reports on rallies in Philadelphia.

179. Three specially printed envelopes express support for the Lincoln–Johnson ticket, which proved victorious in the 1864 election.

181. President Lincoln and son Tad were photographed by Alexander Gardner on February 5, 1865.

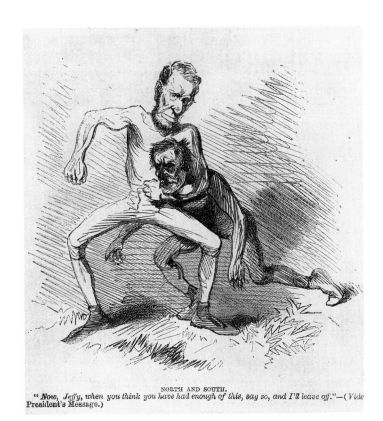

NORTH AND SOUTH.
"*Now, Jeffy, when you think you have had enough of this, say so, and I'll leave off.*"—(*Vide* President's Message.)

180. Lincoln has a stranglehold on Jefferson Davis in this drawing, which first appeared as half of a two-part drawing in *Frank Leslie's Illustrated Newspaper* on December 24, 1864. Northern armies had finally won significant victories, and Christmas 1864 was the last yuletide with the nation divided by war.

182. Lincoln, with his hair cut unusually short, posed for this photograph in early 1865. It was taken by Lewis E. Walker, published by E. and H. T. Anthony of New York.

183. The glass-plate negative of this photograph cracked after a single positive was made on February 5, 1865, and the photographer, Alexander Gardner, destroyed the plate.

184. The crowd awaits the beginning of Lincoln's second inauguration ceremony at the east front of the Capitol on March 4, 1865. Lincoln, on the lower level, is seated to the left of a table on which there is a glass of water; his white collar and shirt are prominent. To his right are Vice-President-elect Andrew Johnson, with crossed legs, and Hannibal Hamlin, the outgoing vice-president. The photographer has not been identified.

185. Lincoln stands at the table reading his second Inaugural Address on March 4, 1865. He holds his address, the shortest any American president has made, in his hand. The photographer is unknown.

INAUGURAL ADDRESS.

MARCH 4, 1865.

FELLOW-COUNTRYMEN: At this second appearing to take the oath of the presidential office, there is less occasion for an extended address than there was at the first. Then, a statement, somewhat in detail, of a course to be pursued, seemed fitting and proper. Now, at the expiration of four years, during which public declarations have been constantly called forth on every point and phase of the great contest which still absorbs the attention and engrosses the energies of the nation, little that is new could be presented. The progress of our arms, upon which all else chiefly depends, is as well known to the public as to myself; and it is, I trust, reasonably satisfactory and encouraging to all. With high hope for the future, no prediction in regard to it is ventured.

On the occasion corresponding to this four years ago, all thoughts were anxiously directed to an impending civil war. All dreaded it—all sought to avert it. While the inaugural address was being delivered from this place, devoted altogether to *saving* the Union without war, insurgent agents were in the city seeking to *destroy* it without war—seeking to dissolve the Union, and divide effects, by negotiation.

186. Lincoln's 1865 Inaugural Address was brief, noble, and most statesmanlike, offering a generous gesture to the South and void of any suggestion of revenge. The peroration or concluding paragraph (not shown) is frequently quoted:

> *With malice toward none; with charity for all; with*
> *firmness in the right, as God gives us to see the right,*
> *let us strive on to finish the work we are in; to bind*
> *the nation's wounds; to care for him who shall have*
> *borne the battle, and for his widow, and his orphan—*
> *to do all which may achieve and cherish a just, and a*
> *lasting peace, among ourselves, and with all nations.*

187. The National Inauguration Ball was held on Monday, March 6, 1865, in three connecting halls of the Patent Office building—one hall for dancing, one for a promenade, and one for dining. Each hall had its own band. President and Mrs. Lincoln and their party spent about two hours at the ball, greeting guests and dining. The revelry did not end until daybreak. More than four thousand tickets were sold. Each ten-dollar ticket admitted one gentleman and two ladies. After expenses were paid, the proceeds were intended to aid soldiers' families, though how much money actually went to them was not recorded. This invitation features etchings of Lincoln and Johnson and lists the ball's many managers.

188. Reputed to be the last portrait of Lincoln painted from life, this oil-on-canvas executed by New Hampshire–born portraitist Joseph Ames was first exhibited to the public on May 15, 1865. The *Boston Transcript* noticed and praised it the same day. It is the property of The Lilly Library.

189. This last photograph of President Lincoln was taken on the day of the inaugural ball by Henry F. Warren, who had schemed to get an opportunity to photograph the president. Warren, uninvited, had photographed Tad Lincoln on his pony and delivered prints to Tad the next day. The boy was delighted and Warren asked for a favor: Would Tad bring his father for a photograph? Tad, who seldom heard his father say no to his requests, reappeared after an interval, with the president at his side. Warren took at least three photographs. After the president's assassination, Warren circulated this one in the form of a carte-de-visite with a legend at the bottom: "The last photograph of PRESIDENT LINCOLN. Taken on the Balcony of the White House March 6, 1865. H. F. WARREN, WALTHAM, MASS."

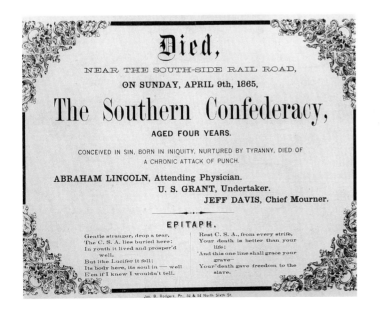

190. The publisher of this broadside considered the surrender of General Robert E. Lee and his Army of Northern Virginia at Appomattox Court House on Sunday, April 9, 1865, to be the end of the Confederacy. Scattered minor resistance continued, but the "stillness at Appomattox" did represent the beginning of the end.

FORD'S THEATRE

TENTH STREET, ABOVE E.

SEASON II....WEEK XXXI....NIGHT 191

WHOLE NUMBER OF NIGHTS, 495.

JOHN T. FORD.............................PROPRIETOR AND MANAGER
(Also of Holliday's St. Theatre, Baltimore, and Academy of Music, Phila)
Stage Manager...J. B. WRIGHT
Treasurer...H. CLAY FORD

Friday Evening, April 14th, 1865.

THIS EVENING

The Performance will be honored by the presence of

PRESIDENT LINCOLN

BENEFIT

—AND—

LAST NIGHT

OF MISS

LAURA KEENE

THE DISTINGUISHED MANAGERESS AUTHORESS, and ACTRESS

Supported by

MR. JOHN DYOTT

AND

MR. HARRY HAWK

TOM TAYLOR'S CELEBRATED ECCENTRIC COMEDY

As originally produced in America by Miss Keene, and performed by her upwards of

ONE THOUSAND NIGHTS,

ENTITLED

OUR AMERICAN

COUSIN

FLORENCE TRENCHARD......MISS LAURA KEENE
(Her Original Character)
Abel Murcott, Clerk to Attorney.....................John Dyott
Asa Trenchard..Harry Hawk
Sir Edward Trenchard..................................T. C. GOURLAY
Lord Dundreary...E. A. EMERSON
Mr. Coyle, Attorney.......................................J. MATTHEWS
Lieutenant Vernon, R. N.............................W. J. FERGUSON
Captain De Boots..C. BYRNES
Binney..G. G. SPEAR
Buddicomb, a Valet.......................................J. H. EVANS
John Whicker, a Gardner................................J. L. DeBONAY
Rasper, a Groom
Bailiffs...................G. A. PARKHURST and L. JOHNSON
Mary Trenchard...Miss J. GOURLAY
Mrs. Mountchessington..................................Mrs. H. MUZZY
Augusta..Miss H. TRUEMAN
Georgiana...Miss M. HART
Sharpe..Mrs. J. H. EVANS
Skillet...Miss M. GOURLAY

SATURDAY EVENING, APRIL 15,

BENEFIT OF MISS JENNIE GOURLAY

When will be presented BOURCICAULT'S Great Sensational Drama,

THE OCTOROON.

Easter Monday, April 17, Engagement of the YOUNG AMERICAN TRAGEDIAN,

EDWIN ADAMS

FOR TWELVE NIGHTS ONLY

THE PRICES OF ADMISSION :
Orchestra..$1.00
Dress Circle and Parquette.................................75
Family Circle...25
Private Boxes...................................$6 and $10
J. R. FORD, Business Manager.

L. Brown, Printer, Washington, D. C.

Death; Funeral; Punishment of Conspirators
(Nos. 191–240)

191. On Friday evening, April 14, 1865, the President and Mrs. Lincoln went to Ford's Theatre in Washington to see *Our American Cousin,* a mediocre comedy written by Tom Taylor, a British dramatist and editor of the British humor magazine *Punch.* This is the playbill.

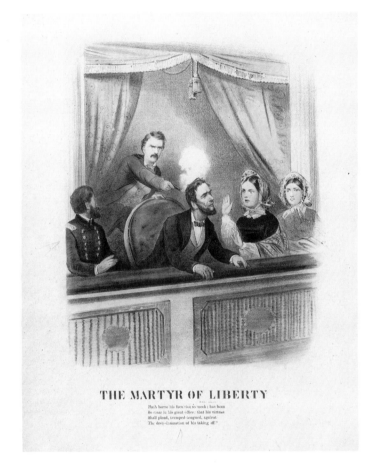

THE MARTYR OF LIBERTY

Hath borne his faculties so meek; has been
So clear in his great office; that his virtues
Shall plead, trumpet-tongued, against
The deep damnation of his taking off."

192. Laura Keene, who played the leading role in *Our American Cousin* on the evening the Lincolns attended Ford's Theatre, was a brilliant actress and the first female producer in the United States. English-born, she moved to New York in 1852 and immediately became a leading lady. In 1856 she built Laura Keene's Theatre, where she was a producer as well as a leading lady until 1863. Following her fateful appearance at Ford's Theatre, she moved to the Chestnut Theatre in Philadelphia but had little success. She died in November 1873.

193. President Lincoln was mortally wounded with a single shot in the back of his head as he sat in a party of four in his box at Ford's Theatre on Tenth Street N.W. in Washington. The time was approximately half-past ten in the evening on Friday, April 14, 1865. Sitting with Lincoln and his wife, Mary, were Major Henry R. Rathbone and Clara Harris, Rathbone's stepsister and fiancée.

The actress Laura Keene held Lincoln's head in her lap while he lay wounded in the theatre. Later, after Lincoln was taken across the street to a small bedroom in the William Petersen home, Miss Keene, along with Miss Harris, tried to console Mrs. Lincoln as her husband lay dying. He died there the following morning, the first president of the United States to be assassinated. This unsigned lithograph, with verses, salutes Lincoln as a "martyr of liberty."

John Wilkes Booth, an actor and fervent southern sympathizer with an unstable personality, was the perpetrator. He had arranged his assassination plan and his escape from Washington during the afternoon and early evening of April 14, and he was successful in both.

194, 195. Major Henry Riggs Rathbone and Clara Harris were guests of the Lincolns in the presidential box at Ford's Theatre the night Lincoln was assassinated. Rathbone attempted to stop the assassin, John Wilkes Booth, and was stabbed in the upper left arm with a dagger. Clara married Rathbone, her stepbrother, two years later, in 1867. In 1887 President Grover Cleveland appointed him consul in Hanover, Germany. There the couple lived with their three children. But Rathbone became mentally ill, killed Clara, and was convicted of the murder by German authorities. Committed to an asylum, he died there in 1911.

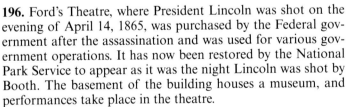

196. Ford's Theatre, where President Lincoln was shot on the evening of April 14, 1865, was purchased by the Federal government after the assassination and was used for various government operations. It has now been restored by the National Park Service to appear as it was the night Lincoln was shot by Booth. The basement of the building houses a museum, and performances take place in the theatre.

197. President Lincoln died at 7:22 on the morning of April 15, 1865, in the William Petersen house on Tenth Street N.W. in Washington. Petersen was a tailor of Swedish ancestry who lived and had his shop in the house and rented extra rooms to boarders. The house was purchased by the Federal government in 1896 and is now administered by the National Park Service.

The room in which Lincoln died was rented to William T. Clark, a Civil War veteran who was a clerk in the quartermaster general's office. The room was small, measuring not more than nine by fifteen feet. Clark continued to rent the room after Lincoln's death, but he experienced difficulties with sightseers. As he wrote his sister in Boston, "Hundreds daily call at the house to gain admission to my room . . . everybody has a great desire to obtain some memento from my room, so that whoever comes in has to be clearly watched for fear they might steal something."

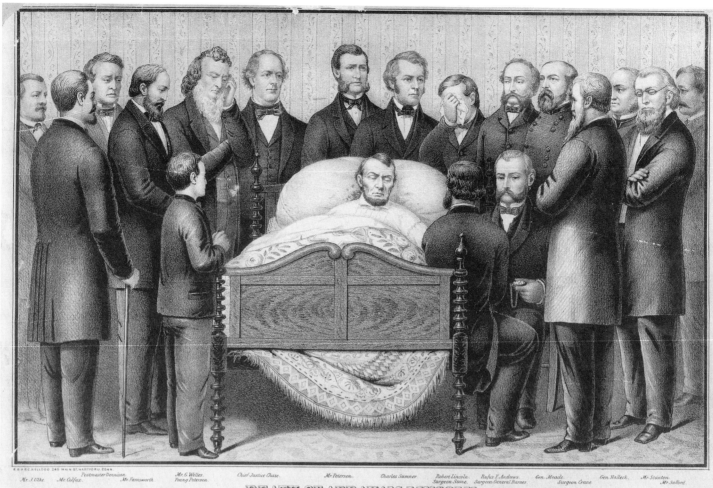

E.B. & E.C. KELLOGG 240 MAIN ST. HARTFORD U. CONN.

| Mr. J. Ulke. | | Postmaster Dennison. | | Mr. G. Welles. | | Chief Justice Chase. | | Mr. Petersen. | | Charles Sumner. | | Robert Lincoln. | | Rufus F. Andrews. | | Gen. Meade. | | Gen. Halleck. | | Mr. Stanton. |
| | Mr. Colfax. | | Mr Farnsworth. | | Young Petersen. | | | | | | | | Surgeon Stone. | | Surgeon General Barnes. | | Surgeon Crane. | | | | Mr. Safford. |

DEATH OF ABRAHAM LINCOLN.
April 15ᵗʰ 1865.

259.

$30,000 REWARD

DESCRIPTION

OF

JOHN WILKES BOOTH!

Who Assassinated the PRESIDENT on the Evening of April 14th, 1865.

Height 5 feet 8 inches; weight 160 pounds; compact built; hair jet black, inclined to curl, medium length, parted behind; eyes black, and heavy dark eye-brows; wears a large seal ring on little finger; when talking inclines his head forward; looks down.

Description of the Person who Attempted to Assassinate Hon. W. H. Seward, Secretary of State.

Height 6 feet 1 inch; hair black, thick, full and straight; no beard, nor appearance of beard; cheeks red on the jaws; face moderately full; 22 or 23 years of age; eyes, color not known—large eyes, not prominent; brows not heavy, but dark; face not large, but rather round; complexion healthy; nose straight and well formed, medium size; mouth small; lips thin; upper lip protruded when he talked; chin pointed and prominent; head medium size; neck short, and of medium length; hands soft and small; fingers tapering; shows no signs of hard labor; broad shoulders; taper waist; straight figure; strong looking man; manner not gentlemanly, but vulgar; Overcoat double-breasted, color mixed of pink and grey spots, small —was a sack overcoat, pockets in side and one on the breast, with lappells or flaps; pants black, common stuff; new heavy boots; voice small and thin, inclined to tenor.

The Common Council of Washington, D. C., have offered a reward of $20,000 for the arrest and conviction of these Assassins, in addition to which I will pay $10,000.

L. C. BAKER,
Colonel and Agent War Department.

198. In *Death of Abraham Lincoln,* a lithograph published by E. B. and E. C. Kellogg of Hartford, Connecticut, many of Washington's luminaries crowd into the small bedroom where Lincoln died. While the scene is imaginary, George Alfred Townsend, special correspondent for the *New York World,* did report that more than twenty-five people were in the room at Lincoln's death, including cabinet members Stanton, Welles, Usher, Speed, and Dennison; Clara Harris, Richard Oglesby, and Lincoln's secretary John Hay; five doctors; and the Reverend Dr. Phineas D. Gurley.

199. John Wilkes Booth was identified as Lincoln's assassin shortly after he jumped from the presidential box onto the Ford's Theatre stage and escaped, riding his horse out of Washington. Lewis Thornton Powell, Booth's co-conspirator who attacked Secretary of State William H. Seward in his home, was arrested at the boardinghouse of Mary Surratt on the night of April 17 as a suspicious-looking character. Later police realized that he was the wanted man described in this broadside.

200, 201. The photograph of a hatless John Wilkes Booth was taken by Charles D. Fredricks of New York about 1862. Fredricks sold it as a carte-de-visite. The one of Booth with hat and cane, also a carte-de-visite, was sold by Case and Getchell of Boston.

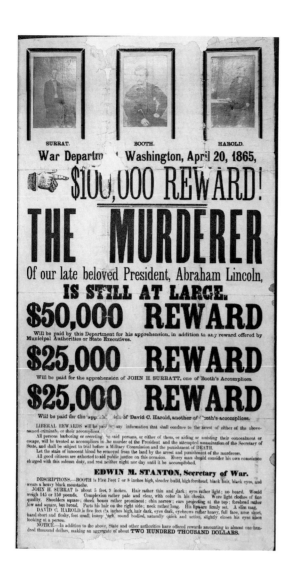

202. This broadside issued by the War Department is considered very rare because it contains photographs of conspirators John Wilkes Booth, David Herold (misspelled here as Harold), and John H. Surratt. Booth was tracked down and mortally wounded on April 26, 1865. Herold, who was with him, surrendered. Surratt, son of the woman who ran the boardinghouse where the assassination plot was thought to have been hatched, fled to Canada, to England, then to the Papal States, where he served as a pontifical Zouave. There he was arrested but escaped to Egypt, where he was recaptured and brought back to the United States to stand trial before a civil court in 1867. The trial lasted two months and resulted in a hung jury. The judge discharged the jury and Surratt went free.

203. (*Below*) When John Wilkes Booth rode out of Washington soon after he shot Lincoln, he was joined by David Herold outside the city. They stopped in Surrattsville, Maryland, for whiskey and a carbine, then rode to the farmhouse of a Dr. Samuel A. Mudd, who made a splint for Booth's leg, which he had fractured when he jumped to the stage of Ford's Theatre. Thomas A. Jones hid them for six days and five nights. They next reached the farm of Richard H. Garrett near Front Royal, Virginia, where they were sleeping in a tobacco barn on the morning of April 26. When surrounded by Union cavalrymen, Herold surrendered, but Booth refused to do so. Sergeant Thomas P. "Boston" Corbett mortally wounded Booth with a single shot. Dragged from the barn, Booth reportedly uttered the words "Tell mother, tell mother, I died for my country," before dying.

This lithograph, published by Charles, Kimmel, and Foster of New York (with misspellings) is titled *Capture of Harrold and the Shooting of Booth in the Barn of Garath's Farm by a detachment of the 16th New York Cavalry under the Order of Col. Baker.*

204. The funeral procession of the dead president was photographed on Pennsylvania Avenue in Washington on April 19, 1865. Government officials wanted to have the body of Lincoln interred in a crypt in the Capitol that had been prepared for the remains of President George Washington but had not been used. A delegation from Springfield hurried to Washington and persuaded Mrs. Lincoln to return Lincoln's body to his Illinois hometown for burial.

After preparation, the body was placed in an open casket and put on view in the East Room of the White House on April 18. Thousands filed by to view the remains. A funeral ceremony, the first of many, was held in the White House on April 19 and was attended by government officials and the diplomatic corps. Robert Todd Lincoln attended the ceremony, but Mary Lincoln and her son Tad were too grief-stricken to be present. At two o'clock in the afternoon, a large hearse carried the body to the Capitol. A procession estimated at 500,000 persons followed the hearse. The open coffin was placed in the rotunda of the Capitol, where the body was on view the remainder of the day and all next day as well.

Secretary of War Stanton decided that the funeral must be military, and he arranged the itinerary of the funeral train that carried the Lincoln remains back to Springfield. It was the reverse of the route Lincoln had followed as president-elect, slightly altered. Cincinnati and Pittsburgh were omitted from the route; Chicago was added. On Friday, April 21, 1865, Lincoln's coffin, along with that of his son, William Wallace "Willie" Lincoln, which had been disinterred, were placed aboard a special train for the slow trip. For twelve days the train traveled the 1,662 miles from Washington to Springfield, making major stops in Baltimore, Harrisburg, Philadelphia, New York, Albany, Buffalo, Cleveland, Columbus, Indianapolis, and Chicago; uncounted thousands viewed the open coffin. Even in villages and small towns the train made short stops of ten minutes. The penultimate stop was in Lincoln, Illinois, the first town named for him, twenty-eight miles northeast of Springfield. In every town on the route, people flocked to the rail side and stood silently in solemn respect to the slain Lincoln. In many towns salutes were fired and bells were tolled. No mighty king or sovereign was ever mourned so intensely for such a prolonged period by so many people.

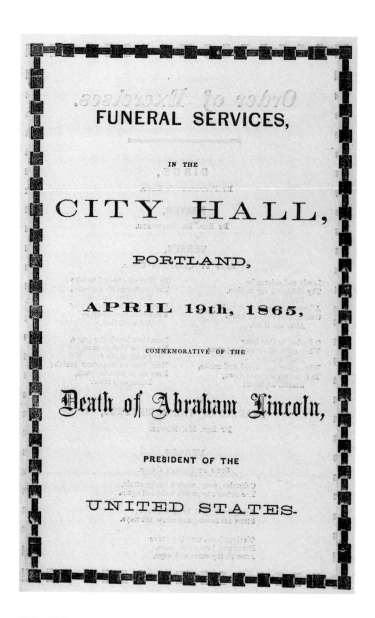

205. This program was for the Lincoln funeral service in Portland, Maine. Hundreds of cities, towns, and villages throughout the North held civil and religious services for the slain president. More than three hundred of these orations and sermons exist in printed form, barometers of the public grief. The Lilly Library collection contains at least 150 of them.

206. The funeral train arrived in Philadelphia at 4:30 P.M. on April 22. The carriage shown in this photograph of the procession at Sixth and Chestnut streets had been constructed specifically for the occasion. It was escorted to Independence Hall through a crowd estimated at a half-million. There Lincoln's body was on view for the better part of two days.

207. A crowd waits to view the body of Lincoln at New York City Hall, April 24. The coffin was taken by ferry across the Hudson River from the train depot in Jersey City, New Jersey, and escorted by the Seventh Regiment of the New York National Guard to City Hall. A writer gave this description:

The procession which followed the remains was in keeping with the funeral car, the whole being indescribably grand and imposing. As far as the eye could see, a dense mass of people, many of them wearing some insignia of mourning, filled the streets and crowded every window. The fronts of the houses were *draped in mourning, and the national ensign displayed at half-mast from the top of almost every building. . . . During the time it was moving, minute guns were fired at different points, and bells were tolled from nearly all the church steeples in the city. The chimes of Trinity church wailed forth the tune of "Old Hundred" in a most solemn and impressive manner.*

The body remained in New York for about thirty hours and was on view for at least twenty-two hours. Reporters estimated that at least 150,000 persons passed the open coffin.

208. This view of Lincoln's funeral procession in New York, redrawn from a photograph by Mathew Brady, is from *Harper's Weekly,* May 13, 1865. A writer described it:

All the beautiful day on Tuesday, when the dearly beloved President was borne through the great city, it was impossible not to feel that however impassioned and tender all the orators might be, no oration could *be so eloquent as the spectacle of the vast population, hushed and bareheaded, under the bright spring sky, gazing upon his coffin. It was one of the most imposing and touching pageants ever seen. From windows and house-tops and balconies, from trees and posts and door-steps, the multitude looked silently on, themselves a striking part of the scene they admired.*

209. *Frank Leslie's Illustrated Newspaper* used many of its artists to draw this scene of the catafalque of the assassinated president as it made its way up flag-draped Broadway in New York on April 25. The scene was published in the newspaper on May 13. According to the paper, nearly a million spectators viewed the parade.

210. This special timetable covers the itinerary of the Lincoln funeral train from Buffalo, New York, to Erie, Pennsylvania. The train arrived in Buffalo at 7:00 A.M. on Thursday, April 27. The coffin was moved to a hearse, which was escorted to St. James Hall. There the body was viewed by an estimated fifty thousand persons. The train departed Buffalo at 10:00 P.M. and reached Erie early the following morning after making seventeen ten-minute stops at towns along the route.

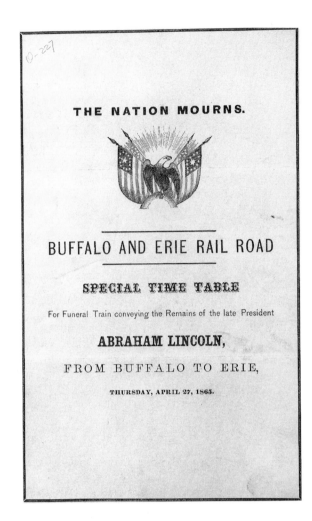

211. This funeral carriage conveyed Lincoln's coffin from the railroad station to the Indiana Statehouse in Indianapolis. It was drawn by eight white horses, including six that had drawn the carriage in which President-elect Lincoln rode as he visited Indianapolis on his way to Washington in 1861. The funeral train arrived in the city at 7:00 A.M. on Sunday, April 30. An elaborate program had been planned, but incessant rain forced its cancellation. Delegations from Cincinnati and from many towns in Indiana and Kentucky were there to take part in a grand parade, which also was called off. But thousands of persons nonetheless paid silent respect as they filed past the open coffin in the Statehouse.

212. The Indiana Statehouse draped for the Lincoln obsequies on April 30. Governor Oliver P. Morton had planned to deliver a public eulogy, but it was cancelled owing to the foul weather. The funeral train left for Chicago near midnight.

213. The Lincoln funeral train arrived in Chicago at 11:00 A.M. on May 1. It stopped at Park Place, where this great triple arch had been erected to serve as the beginning point of a huge military parade to the Courthouse. The arches, decorated with American flags, portraits of Lincoln, and an American eagle, contained three inscriptions. "We honor Him Dead who honored Us while Living," "Rest in peace noble soul, patriot heart," and "Faithful to Right. A Martyr to Justice."

The girls, all dressed in white and banded with crepe, were from a Chicago high school. They walked around the bier, and each girl deposited flowers on the coffin in passing.

The procession of military men and ranking civilians to the Courthouse was described as

> . . . *a wilderness of banners and flags, with their mottoes and inscriptions. The estimated number of persons in line was thirty thousand, and there were three times as many more who witnessed the procession by crowding into the streets bordering on the line of march, making about one hundred and fifty thousand who were on the streets of Chicago that day. . . .*

Lincoln's body was on view in the rotunda of the Courthouse for sixteen hours, and a huge crowd was still waiting to get in when the doors were closed.

214. The Chicago and Alton Railroad depot in Springfield was photographed on May 3, the day the Lincoln funeral train arrived. The arrival time was 9:00 A.M.—just one hour later than the scheduled time, after traveling twelve days and 1,662 miles. A hearse, drawn by six black horses draped in black, transported the coffin from the depot to the Illinois Statehouse. The hearse had also been used in 1858 for the funeral of Senator Thomas Hart Benton in St. Louis.

215. The Lincoln home in Springfield, draped for Lincoln's funeral, was photographed on May 3 or 4, 1865. "Old Bob," Lincoln's horse, was brought out of retirement to stand before the house in a mourning blanket.

216. The Illinois Statehouse in Springfield was decorated for Lincoln's funeral with "about fifteen hundred yard of black and white goods. . . . Evergreen and flowers, interwoven with crepe, hung in festoons from capitals, columns and cornices in all parts of the building." This building, the fifth statehouse in Illinois, served as the Capitol from 1839 to 1876. Lincoln served here as a state representative, practiced before the Illinois Supreme Court in this structure, presented his "House Divided" speech here in 1858, and used offices here after becoming president-elect.

217. Lincoln's body lay in state in the Illinois Hall of Representatives on May 3 and 4. This photograph shows the crowd waiting to enter the building to view the body. One account states that "from the time the coffin was opened, at ten o'clock on the morning of May third, there was no cessation of visitors. All through the still hours of the night, no human voices were heard except in subdued tones, as men and women filed through the State House. . . ."

218. Major General Joseph Hooker is listed as marshal in chief in this printed "Order of Funeral Procession" for President Lincoln in Springfield on Thursday, May 4, 1865. Thousands poured into Springfield for the last rites of its most famous resident. After the body lay in state for twenty-six hours, the coffin was sealed at noon on May 4, and the funeral procession, led by General Hooker, began its slow march to Oak Ridge Cemetery at the northern outskirts of Springfield.

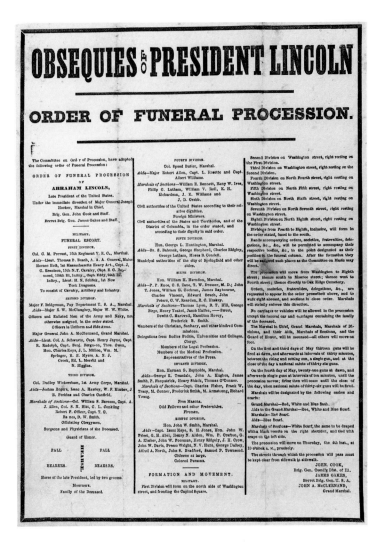

219. (*Below*) This proclamation was issued by Lincoln's successor, President Andrew Johnson, on May 2, 1865. Many persons in and out of the Federal government thought the assassination of Lincoln was a conspiracy of the crumbling Confederate government. Secretary of War Edwin Stanton, who took charge of U.S. government operations while Lincoln lay on his deathbed, thought the assassination plot was hatched in Richmond, the Confederate capital. Radical Republicans in Congress used the assassination as an excuse to seek vengeance on the seceded states. The Confederate president, Jefferson Davis, was not involved; nor were any officials of the Confederate states. But the conspirators did include ex-Confederate soldiers who were filled with hatred of the North and sympathy for the cause of the South. Though signed by President Johnson, this proclamation probably was inspired by Stanton. The men named in the proclamation were former Confederate agents who had fled to Canada.

Head-Quarters Cavalry Corps M. D. M.

Macon, May 8th, 1865.

The following Proclamation is published for the information and government of the command:

PROCLAMATION

BY THE PRESIDENT.

Whereas it appears from evidence in the Bureau of Military Justice, that the atrocious murder of the late President and the attempted murder of the Hon. William H. Seward, Secretary of State, was incited and concerted by and between Jeff Davis, late of Richmond and Jacob Thompson, Clement C. Clay, Beverly Tucker, George N. Sanders, W. C. Cleary and others, rebels and traitors against the Government of the United States, harbored in Canada. Now, therefore, to the end that justice may be done.

I, ANDREW JOHNSON, President of the United States, do offer for the arrest of said persons, or either of them, within the limits of the United States, that they be brought to trial, the following reward: $100,000 for the arrest of Jeff. Davis: $100,000 for the arrest of Clement C. Clay; $100,000 for the arrest of Jacob Thompson, late of Mississippi; $25,000 for the arrest of Geo. N. Sanders; $25,000 for the arrest of Beverly Tucker; and $10,000 for the arrest of W. C. Cleary, late Clerk of C. C.

The Provost Marshal General of the United States is directed to cause a description of said persons, with notice of the above rewards, to be published.

In testimony whereof, I have hereunto set my hand and caused the seal of the United States to be affixed. Done at the City of Washington, 2d day of May, in the year of our Lord, 1865, and of Independence of the United States of America 88th.

(Signed)   ANDREW JOHNSON.

W. HUNTER, Acting Secretary of State.

In order to secure the arrest of the above named parties, the greatest activity and vigilance is enjoined upon the officers and men of the Cavalry Corps.

By command of BR'V'T MAJ. GEN. WILSON.

     E. B. BEAUMONT, Major & A. A. Gen.

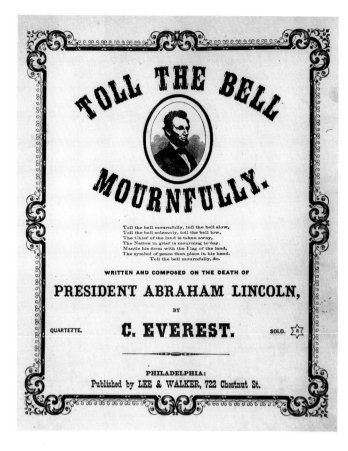

220–227. The death of President Lincoln brought forth an unprecedented cascade of music and song expressing the nation's grief. Professional and amateur composers were moved to relieve the sorrow in compositions of varied quality and form—dirges, marches, hymns of grief. Publishers obligingly supplied the market's demands. Shown here are the sheet-music covers of eight representative compositions.

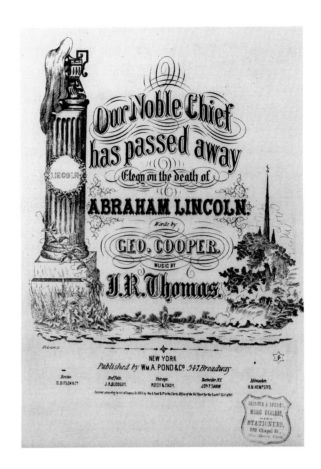

228. These envelopes circulated after Lincoln's death.

229. The lithograph *Uncle Sam's Menagerie* was published on June 7, 1865, before completion of the trial of the persons accused of conspiring to assassinate Lincoln. It suggests that all of the conspirators be sent to the gallows, along with the "Hyena," Jefferson Davis. Thus it seems to suggest that Davis had something to do with the assassination. He did not. The conspirators were acting alone, and their actions were not part of a southern conspiracy. The lithographer misspelled the names of Herold and Atzerodt.

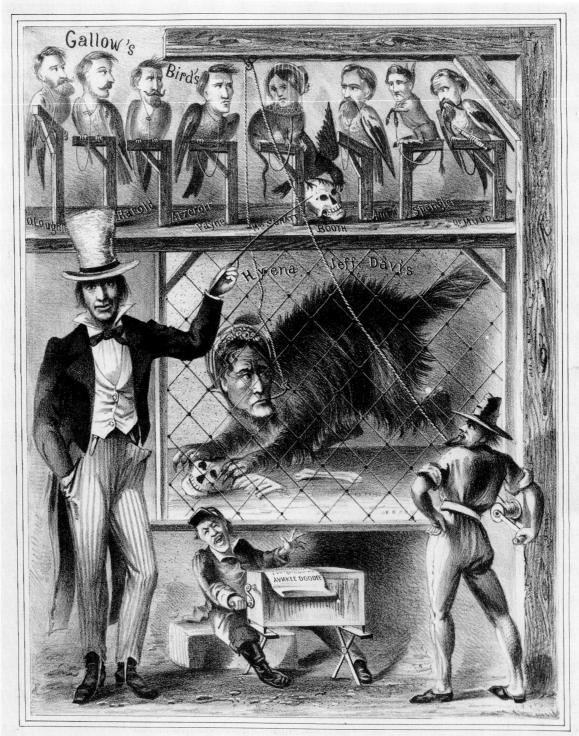

230. A nine-member military commission composed of army officers tried John Wilkes Booth's male accomplices and Mary E. Surratt in Washington from May 10 to June 30, 1865. The nine officers shown in this photograph are David R. Clendenin, James A. Ekin, Robert S. Foster, T. M. Harris, Alvin P. Howe, David Hunter, C. H. Tompkins, August V. Kautz, and Lew Wallace. Also in the photograph, at far right, is Joseph Holt, judge advocate general and chief prosecutor at the trial. To his right are Henry L. Burnett and John A. Bingham, assistant prosecutors. The jurisdiction of the military commission was questionable. Fear and a desire for revenge led the Johnson Administration to ignore the protests of lawyers and citizens who contended that the military had no jurisdiction over the conspirators.

Defendants George Atzerodt, David E. Herold, Lewis Thornton Powell, and Mrs. Surratt were found guilty and were hanged together on July 7 in Washington's Capitol Prison. Defendants Samuel B. Arnold, Michael O'Laughlin, and Dr. Samuel A. Mudd were sentenced to life in prison. Edman Spangler, an employee at Ford's Theatre who briefly held Booth's horse, was given six years at hard labor. Spangler, Arnold, and Mudd were pardoned by President Johnson in 1869. O'Laughlin died in prison of yellow fever in 1867. A ninth defendant, John H. Surratt, fled the country but was captured, brought back, and tried by a civil court in 1867. The trial resulted in a hung jury, and he went free.

231. George A. Atzerodt, a German-born wagon painter, was assigned by John Wilkes Booth to kill Vice-President Andrew Johnson on April 14, 1865. He lost his nerve and fled to western Maryland, where he was arrested on April 20. Found guilty in the conspiracy, he was hanged on July 7. Atzerodt also participated along with Powell, Herold, John Surratt, and two former Confederate soldiers in Booth's unsuccessful plot to abduct Lincoln in March 1865.

232, 233. Widow Mary E. Surratt moved to Washington from Surrattsville, Maryland, in 1864 and became the proprietress of this eight-room boardinghouse on H Street, N.W., which the conspirators Booth, Powell, and Atzerodt were known to have visited. On the slimmest of evidence, the military commission found Mrs. Surratt guilty of conspiracy and sentenced her to hang. Even though five members of the commission recommended clemency because of her sex, she was hanged on July 7, 1865. President Johnson maintained that he never saw the recommendation.

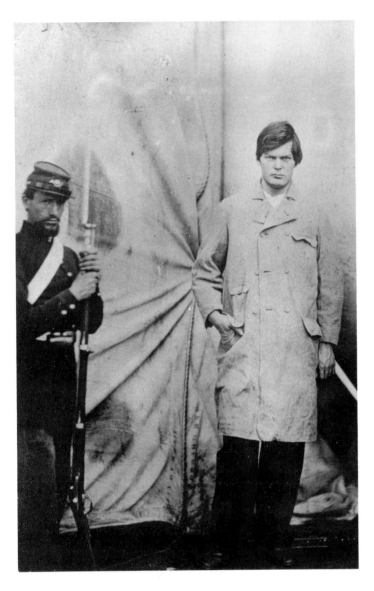

234. Lewis Thornton Powell (also known as Lewis Paine) is shown here in a photograph taken after his arrest. As a Confederate infantryman and cavalryman, Powell had been wounded and taken prisoner at Gettysburg. In January 1865 he took an oath of allegiance to the United States and went to Baltimore to live. He somehow met Booth and received money from him for living expenses. On April 14, assigned by Booth to kill Secretary of State William H. Seward, he sought entrance to Seward's home by posing as a messenger bringing medicine from Seward's doctor for the convalescing Seward. Refused entry, Powell knocked Seward's son Frederick unconscious with a pistol; stabbed the secretary of state several times and also stabbed his male nurse; knocked down another son, Augustus; and wounded a State Department messenger. He made his escape on horseback. On April 17 he was arrested at the door of Mary Surratt's boardinghouse. He was hanged on July 7.

235. David E. Herold, a former pharmacist's clerk with a mental age of about twelve years, fled Washington on the night of the assassination and accidentally met the fleeing Booth. He remained with Booth and surrendered to Federal troops on April 26 near Front Royal, Virginia.

236. The four convicted conspirators stand on the scaffold in Capitol Prison just a few minutes before the trapdoor was sprung on July 7, 1865.

237. Hanging from the scaffold, left to right, are Mary E. Surratt, Lewis T. Powell, David E. Herold, and George A. Atzerodt.

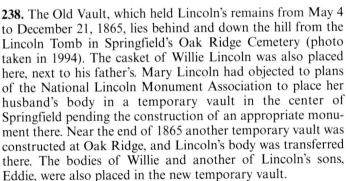

238. The Old Vault, which held Lincoln's remains from May 4 to December 21, 1865, lies behind and down the hill from the Lincoln Tomb in Springfield's Oak Ridge Cemetery (photo taken in 1994). The casket of Willie Lincoln was also placed here, next to his father's. Mary Lincoln had objected to plans of the National Lincoln Monument Association to place her husband's body in a temporary vault in the center of Springfield pending the construction of an appropriate monument there. Near the end of 1865 another temporary vault was constructed at Oak Ridge, and Lincoln's body was transferred there. The bodies of Willie and another of Lincoln's sons, Eddie, were also placed in the new temporary vault.

239. The Lincoln Tomb with its 135-foot shaft in the Oak Ridge Cemetery in Springfield was designed by Larkin G. Mead of Brattleboro, Vermont. The National Lincoln Monument Association raised funds for the tomb's construction, which started in 1869. It was dedicated five years later. Renovation work was done in 1899 and 1930. The works of many artists in addition to Mead adorn the tomb: Gutzon Borglum, Leonard Crunelle, Daniel Chester French, Augustus Saint-Gaudens, Lorado Taft, Fred M. Torrey, and Adolph A. Weinman.

In 1895, the National Lincoln Monument Association gave the tomb to the State of Illinois, and it is now administered by the Illinois Historic Preservation Agency. Mary Todd Lincoln and three of the Lincoln children are also interred in the tomb: Eddie, Willie, and Tad. The oldest son, Robert Todd Lincoln, is buried in Arlington National Cemetery.

240. The central panel, one of the five, at the Visitor Center of the Lincoln Boyhood National Memorial in Spencer County, Indiana (see Nos. 10–13), was carved by E. H. Daniels. *And Now He Belongs to the Ages*, historic words said to have been uttered by Lincoln's Secretary of War, Edwin M. Stanton, at the time of Lincoln's death on April 15, 1865, are a reminder of the heritage the fallen leader left to his countrymen. To the left are the farmer, the laborer, the family, and the freedman—people to whom Lincoln will forever belong. To the right are Clio, muse of history, holding a scroll, and Columbia, holding a wreath of laurel. A cabin and the White House can be seen in the background.

Index
The numbers refer to the illustration numbers (1–240), not to pages.

A.B.C. schools, 1, 5
Adams, John Quincy, 100
Alabama, 65, 105, 141
    Montgomery, 105
Alschuler, Samuel G., 45, 99
American Anti-Slavery Society, 80
American party, 64
Ames, Joseph, 188
Anderson, Robert, 122
Anderson River, 5
Angle, Paul, 44
Anthony, E. and H. T., 154, 182
Antietam, 139, 140
Antietam, Battle of, 139, 156
Appomattox Court House, 13, 127, 128, 190
Arkansas, 65, 122, 141
Arlington National Cemetery, 127, 128, 239
Armstrong, Duff, 46
Arnold, Samuel B., 230
Arthur, Chester A., 127, 128
Art Institute of Chicago, 36
Atwood, Jesse, 100
Atzerodt, George A., 229–233, 236, 237

Babcock, James F., 35
Baken, J. E., 162, 174
Baker, Colonel, 203
Ball, George A., 149, 150
Barr, J. E., 100
Barrett, Oliver R., 8
Bates, Edward, 118, 119
Beauregard, Pierre G. T., 122, 164
Beckel, J. D., 124–126
Bedell, Grace, 99
Beecher, Henry Ward, 122
Bell, John, 59, 64, 79, 85, 86, 88, 90–92, 95, 97, 98, 145
Benton, Senator Thomas Hart, 214
Berger, Anthony, 153
Berry, William F., 16, 24, 25
Bingham, John A., 230
Black Hawk War, 16, 22, 27
Blair, Montgomery, 118, 119, 175
Blanchard, W. S., 166
Blondin, Charles, 95
books
    Abraham Lincoln: A History, 111, 112
    Collected Works of Abraham Lincoln, The, 7
    German-language edition of a Lincoln biography, 77
    Herndon's Lincoln: The True Story of a Great Life, 31
    Kentucky Preceptor, The, 8
    Life of Abraham Lincoln, 76
    Lincoln in Photographs, 48
    "Wigwam Edition" of a Lincoln biography, 75
    With Malice Toward None: The Life of Abraham Lincoln, 76
Booth, John Wilkes, 193–196, 199–203, 230–235
Borglum, Gutzon, 239
Brady, Mathew B., 59, 68, 113, 114, 124–126, 129, 130, 133, 139, 208
    and Company, 119
    Gallery, 152, 153
Bragg, Braxton, 170
Breckinridge, John C., 59, 62, 65, 79, 84, 85, 90–95, 97, 98
Brown, John, 142
Brown, John Henry, 60
Browning, Orville H., 12
Bryant, William Cullen, 136, 137
Buchanan, James, 89, 91–94

Burleigh, William Henry, 80
Burnett, Henry L., 230
Burnside, Ambrose E., 139
Butler, Preston, 47, 60, 101
Buttre, J. C., 118
Byers, Abraham, 46

cabinet, Lincoln's, 118, 119, 158, 175
California, 98, 155
Cameron, Simon, 56, 118
campaign literature, 73–75, 83, 167–170, 176–179
    Lincoln Catechism, The, 172
    National Union League Gazette, 178
    Platforms, The, 155
    Rail Splitter, The, 78
    Republican Pocket Pistol, The, 80
    Running the "Machine," 158
Carpenter, Francis Bicknell, 149, 150
cartoons, 67, 91, 93, 98, 120, 161–164, 174
    Abraham's Dream!, 157
    Father Abraham, 171
    Little Game of Bagatelle, A, 160
    National Union League Gazette, 178
    Platforms Illustrated, 173
    Political "Blondins" Crossing Salt River, 95
    Political Gymnasium, The, 90
    Political Quadrille, The, 92
    Political Race, A, 97
    Slow & Steady Wins the Race, 163
    Storming the Castle, 94
    "The Schoolmaster Abroad" at Last, 121
    Universal Advice to Abraham. Drop 'Em!, 143
    Your Plan and Mine, 159
Case and Getchell, 200, 201
Cass County Courthouse, 46
Chapman, Harriet Hanks, 49
Charles, Kimmel, and Foster, 203
Chase, Salmon Portland, 56, 118, 155, 158
Chicago and Alton Railroad, 214
Chicago Courthouse, 213
Church, J., 82
Civil War, 59, 116, 122, 124–126, 134, 136, 137, 141, 156, 160
Clark, William T., 197
Clendenin, David R., 230
Cleveland, Grover, 194, 195
Cochrane, John, 175
Confederate Army, 139, 145, 156, 170, 190
Confederate States of America, 59, 62, 105, 120, 122, 141, 142, 155, 159, 164, 190, 219
Connecticut, 56, 88, 118
    Hartford, 198
Constitutional Union party, 59, 64, 86, 88, 98
Cooke and Fassett, 54
Cooper Institute, 56, 59, 68
copperhead, 142, 170, 173
Corbett, Thomas P., 203
Correll, Ira A., 14
Coster, Robert, 133, 154
Crawford, Andrew, 5
Crawford, Elizabeth, 8
Crawford, Josiah, 8, 11
Crunelle, Leonard, 22, 43, 239
C-SPAN, 40
Cuba, 65
Cunningham, Judge & Mrs. J. O., 36
Currier & Ives, 67, 68, 70, 84, 85, 90, 91, 93–95, 120, 132, 157–159, 161, 164, 175

Daniels, Elmer Harland, 10, 240
Davis, David, 56

Davis, Jefferson, 105, 120, 159, 161, 164, 165, 180, 219, 229
Day, Ben, 67, 120, 132
Declaration of Independence, 42
Delaware, 65, 155
Democratic party, 59, 62, 64, 65, 93, 155, 160, 161, 170
    1860 National Convention, 65
    1864 National Convention, 155, 160, 170, 173
    platform, 155, 160, 163
    presidential candidates, 59, 62, 65, 93, 155–157, 160, 161, 163–165
Dennison, William, 119, 198
District of Columbia, 133
Ditson, Oliver, 166
Dix, John A., 158
Dorsey, Azel W., 5
Douglas, Mrs. Stephen A. (Adele Cutts), 61
Douglas, Stephen Arnold, 26, 27, 39–41, 42, 45, 59, 62, 84, 85, 86, 88, 90, 91, 93–95, 97, 98
Dred Scott Decision, 86
Dred Scott v. Sandford, 92
Dresser, Charles, 71
Dubois, Jesse, 56

Early, Jubal Anderson, 170
Ecole des Beaux-Arts, 36
Ehrgott, Forbriger, & Company, 82
Ekin, James A., 230
Electoral College, 59, 62, 64, 65, 155
Ellsworth, Elmer Ephraim, 124–126
Emancipation Proclamation, 67, 132, 141, 142, 149, 150, 155
Everett, Edward, 64, 90, 95, 145, 146

Fairbanks, Avard Tennyson, 21, 42
Farragut, David, 155, 173
Fassett, Samuel M., 54, 81, 82
Feeks, J. F., 172
Fell, Jesse W., 5, 56
Fessenden, William Pitt, 158
Fire Zouaves, 124–126
Fisher, Clara V., 100
Florida, 65, 105
Follett and Foster, 40
Ford's Theatre, 191–196, 199, 203, 230
Fort Dixon, 22
Fort Johnson, 122
Fort Sumter, 122, 123
Foster, Robert S., 230
Francis, Simon, 12
Fredricks, Charles D., 200, 201
Frémont, John C., 39, 175
French, Daniel Chester, 239

Gage, Robert Merrill, 37
Gardner, Alexander, 139, 140, 181, 183
Garfield, James A., 127, 128
Garrett, Richard H., 203
Garrison, William Lloyd, 122
Gentry, Allen, 5, 11
Gentry, James, 5, 11
Georgia, 65, 98, 105, 141
    Atlanta, 155
Gettysburg, Battle of, 145, 234
Gettysburg Address, 146
Gettysburg National Cemetery, 145–148
Gibbons, James Sloan, 136, 137
Gilmer, D. H., 50
Globe Tavern, 101
Graham, Christopher Columbus, 10

Grant, Ulysses S., 13, 127, 128, 160, 164, 170, 173
Great Western Railroad, 71, 108, 109
Greeley, Horace, 70, 75, 90, 95, 141
Grigsby, Aaron, 11
Gurley, Phineas D., 198

Hale, Sarah Josepha, 144
Hall, Matilda Johnston, 16
Hall, Squire Levi, 16
Halleck, Henry W., 132, 143
Hamilton and Ostendorf, 48
Hamlin, Hannibal, 63, 77, 93, 118, 184
Hanks, Dennis F., 11, 16, 17, 49
Hanks, Elizabeth Johnston, *see* Johnston, Elizabeth
Hanks, John, 16, 17, 78
Hanks, Nancy, *see* Lincoln, Nancy Hanks
Harris, Clara, 193–195, 198
Harris, T. M., 230
Harrison, Benjamin, 127, 128
Harvard University, 127, 128
Hay, John Milton, 111, 112, 198
Hazel, Caleb, 1, 10
Hearst, William Randolph, 20
Helmsmuller, F. B., 138
Hering, Henry, 15
Herndon, James, 24
Herndon, Rowan, 24
Herndon, William Henry, 5, 7, 8, 12, 31, 34
Herold, David E., 202, 203, 229–231, 235, 237
Herron School of Art, 9
Hesler, Alexander, 35, 79
Higgins, H. M., 81
Hilyard, Thomas J., 38
Holt, Joseph, 230
Hooker, Joseph, 218
Howe, Alvin P., 230
Hudson River, 207
Hunter, David, 230
Huntington, Anna Hyatt, 20

Illinois, 14, 16, 17, 20, 33, 59, 62, 72, 84, 97–99, 168, 216, 239
  Alton, 40
  Atlanta, 47
  Beardstown, 16, 46
  Bloomington, 5, 39
  Cass County, 46
  Champaign, 44
  Champaign County, 36
  Charleston, 40, 106, 107
  Chicago, 8, 30, 35, 37, 40, 48, 54, 56, 58, 62, 66, 78, 79, 81, 87, 99, 100, 124–128, 131, 134, 155, 160, 173, 204, 212, 213
    Bryan Hall, 124–126
    Clifton House, 101
    Courthouse, 213
    Park Place, 213
  Clinton, 26
    Mr. Lincoln Square, 26
  Coles County, 7, 17, 106, 107
  Danville, 38
  Decatur, 16–19, 78
    Fairview Park, 17
    Harrell's Tavern, 19
    Lincoln Square, 19
  DeWitt County, 26
  Dixon, 22
  Edgar County, 73
  Elmwood, 36
  Freeport, 40, 41
    Debate Square, 41
    Taylor's Park, 43
  Galesburg, 40, 42
  Jacksonville, 62
  Jonesboro, 40

Kaskaskia, 29
Knox County, 42
Lincoln, 37, 204
Logan County, 37
Macon County, 16, 17, 78
Menard County, 16
Monmouth, 51, 52
New Salem, 16, 20, 22, 24, 25, 31, 46
  New Salem State Park, 20, 21, 23
Ottawa, 40
Paris, 73
Pekin, 176
Peoria, 36, 52
Petersburg, 20
Pittsfield, 50, 52
Quincy, 40, 44
  Washington Park, 44
Sangamon County, 16, 29
Sangamon Town, 16
Springfield, 3, 12, 16, 18, 27, 29–33, 37, 40, 47, 49, 52, 56, 60, 71, 87, 99–102, 103, 107–112, 124–129, 204, 214–216, 218, 238, 239
  Tinsley Building, 30, 31, 34
Stockton, 41
Urbana, 36, 45
  Carle Park, 36
Vandalia, 25, 29
  Illinois Statehouse, 29
Vermilion County, 38
Virginia, 46
Illinois Central Railroad, 36
Illinois Eighth Judicial Circuit, 26, 31, 36, 37
Illinois General Assembly, 25, 27–29, 110
Illinois Hall of Representatives, 217
Illinois Historic Preservation Agency, 29, 106, 239
Illinois House of Representatives, 24, 25
Illinois Seventh Congressional District, 33
Illinois State Historical Library, 27, 30, 139
Illinois Statehouse, 29, 30, 110, 214, 216, 217
Illinois State Supreme Court, 31, 216
Illinois State University, 127, 128
Inaugural Address
  first, 115, 122, 185, 186
  second, 185, 186
Indiana, 1, 3, 5, 6, 8, 14, 16, 84, 98, 107, 155, 168–170, 211
  Daviess County, 14
  Fort Wayne, 119
  Gentryville, 5
  Indianapolis, 9, 15, 73, 113, 118, 204, 211
    Government Place, 9
    University Park, 15
  Lincoln City, 5
  Muncie, 149, 150
  Odon, 14
    Old Settlers Park, 14
  Perry County, 5
  Rockport, 11
  South Bend, 6
  Spencer County, 5, 6, 10, 240
    Lincoln Ferry Park, 15
  Terre Haute, 73, 119
  Troy, 5
  Vincennes, 16
Indiana Government Center, 9
Indiana Lincoln Union, 6
Indiana Statehouse, 9, 211, 212
Indiana University, 8, 9, 100, 149, 150
Iowa, 98
Iowa Territory, 22

Jackson, Andrew, 16, 25, 155
Jackson, Calvin, 50
James Millikin University, 18
Jefferson Memorial, 1

Johnson, Andrew, 155, 162, 176, 184, 187, 219, 230–233
Johnson, Herschel, 93
Johnston, Elizabeth, 11, 16, 49, 107
Johnston, John D., 16, 17, 107
Johnston, Matilda, 16, 106, 107
Johnston, Sarah Bush, *see* Lincoln, Sarah Bush Johnston
Jones, Thee, 78
Jones, Thomas A., 203
Jordan, J. H., 78
Joslin, Amon T., 38
Judd, Norman B., 56

Kansas, 87
Kautz, August V., 230
Keene, Laura, 192, 193
Kellogg, E. B. & E. C., 198
Kentucky, 1–5, 14, 16, 59, 64, 65, 98, 119, 155, 211
  Elizabethtown, 5, 107
  Harden County, 1
  Hodgenville, 1–3
  Larue County, 1
  Lexington, 101
Knob Creek, 4, 10
Knox College, 42

LaFollette, Jesse, 10
LaFollette, Robert, 10
Lamon, Ward Hill, 56
Lane, Joseph, 65, 93, 95
Lebold, Foreman M., 7, 8
Lee, Robert E., 127, 128, 139, 156, 164, 190
Lee & Walker, 81
Leverick v. Leverick, 38
Library of Congress, 111, 112
Lilly Library, 7, 40, 80, 100, 149, 150, 154, 188, 205
Lincoln, Abraham, writings of, 5, 7, 16, 99, 124–126, 135, 141, 146, 155, 186
Lincoln, Abraham "Jack" (grandson), 127, 128
Lincoln, Edward Baker "Eddie" (son), 101, 238, 239
Lincoln, Jesse Harlan (grandson), 127, 128
Lincoln, Mary (granddaughter), 127, 128
Lincoln, Mary Eunice (née Harlan; daughter-in-law), 127, 128
Lincoln, Mary Todd (wife), 12, 27, 31, 71, 72, 87, 101, 102, 104, 129, 130, 133, 149, 150, 154, 187, 191, 193, 204, 238, 239
Lincoln, Nancy Hanks (mother), 1, 6, 10, 78
Lincoln, Robert Todd (son), 3, 72, 101, 111, 112, 127, 128, 204, 239
Lincoln, Sarah (sister; Mrs. Aaron Grigsby), 4, 6, 10
Lincoln, Sarah Bush Johnston (stepmother), 5, 7, 11, 16, 49, 106, 107
Lincoln, Thomas (father), 1, 5, 10, 16, 106, 107
Lincoln, Thomas, Jr. (brother), 4
Lincoln, Thomas "Tad" (son), 71, 87, 101, 102, 130, 131, 152, 181, 189, 204, 239
Lincoln, William Wallace "Willie" (son), 71, 87, 101, 103, 130, 131, 154, 204, 238, 239
Lincoln Birthplace National Historic Site, 1
Lincoln Boyhood National Memorial, 5, 6, 10, 240
Lincoln College, 37
Lincoln–Douglas Debates, 40, 41, 42, 44, 45, 56, 96
Lincoln Farm Association, 1, 2
Lincoln Heritage Trail, 16
Lincoln Home National Historic Site, 72
Lincoln Log Cabin State Historic Site, 106
Lincoln Memorial, 1, 2
Lincoln Papers, 111, 112

Lincoln Tomb, 3, 18, 22, 27, 36, 43, 238, 239
lithographs, 68, 70, 84, 85, 88, 193 (see also cartoons)
   Breaking That "Backbone," 132
   Capture of Harrold and the Shooting of
      Booth in the Barn of Garath's Farm by
      a detachment of the 16th New York
      Cavalry under the Order of Col.
      Baker, 203
   Death of Abraham Lincoln, 198
   Grand Banner of the Radical Democracy, 175
   Republican Banner for 1860, The, 67
   Uncle Sam's Decision, 90
   Uncle Sam's Menagerie, 229
   Undecided Political Prize Fight, The, 96
Little Pigeon Creek Baptist Church Cemetery,
   6
Logan, David, 30
Logan, Stephen Trigg, 12, 30, 56
Long, Henry C., 15
Louisiana, 105, 141
   New Orleans, 5, 11, 16, 17, 23
Louisiana Territory, 96

Madison, Dolly, 61
Magee, J. L., 160
Maine, 61, 88
   Portland, 205
Maine House of Representatives, 63
Maryland, 65, 118, 139, 231
   Baltimore, 113, 142, 155, 157, 204, 234
   Sharpsburg, 139
   Surrattsville, 203, 232, 233
Massachusetts, 64, 88, 173
   Boston, 71, 122, 166, 197, 200, 201
   Waltham, 189
Maurer, Louis, 67
McClellan, Ellen Mary Marcy, 156
McClellan, George Brinton, 132, 139, 155–157,
   159–161, 163–165, 170, 173
McClernand, John A., 140
McCulloch, Hugh, 119
McGinnis v. Illinois Central Railroad, 36
McKeehan, J. B., 78
Mead, Larkin G., 239
Mendel, Ed., 124–126
Mexican War, 33
Michigan, 98
Minnesota, 98
Mississippi, 65, 105
Missouri, 62, 118
   Hannibal, 52
   St. Louis, 214
Missouri Compromise, 96
Mobile Bay, 155
Monmouth Republication Glee Club, 51
Moore, Matilda Johnston Hall, 106
Moore, Reuben, 106
Morgan, Nicholas C., Sr., 21
Morton, Oliver P., 212
Mudd, Samuel A., 203, 230
Music sheets, 66, 220–227
   "Battle Cry of Freedom, The," 134
   "Give Thanks, all ye People," 144
   "Honest Old Abe," 79
   "Liberty's Call or Hurrah for Abe and
      Andy," 166
   "Lincoln Quick Step," 81, 82
   "Monody," 124–126
   "Our National Union March," 135
   "President Lincoln's Grand March," 138
   "Requiem March," 124–126
   "We are Coming Father Abra'am," 136, 137
   "'Wigwam' Grand March, The," 66

Nancy Hank Lincoln Park, 6
National Arts Foundation, 20

National Gallery of Art, 1
National Guard, New York Seventh Regiment,
   207
National Inaugural Ball, 187, 189
National Lincoln Monument Assocation, 27,
   238, 239
National Park Service, 1, 5, 6, 72, 196, 197
National Portrait Gallery, 60
National Register of Historic Places, 4
National Retail Goods Assocation, 144
National Society of Utah Pioneers, 21
New Hampshire, 56, 88, 127, 128, 188
New Jersey, 62, 64, 65, 155
   Jersey City, 207
   Newark, 83, 167
Newspapers
   Boston Transcript, 188
   Daily Chicago Post, 115
   Decatur Herald and Review, 17
   Evening Post, 136, 137
   Frank Leslie's Illustrated Newspaper, 180,
      209
   London Times, 120, 173
   New York Enquirer, 70, 90
   New York Morning Courier, 70, 90
   New York Times, 70
   New York Tribune, 70, 75, 90, 141
   New York World, 198
   Sangamon Journal, 12
New York, 62, 64, 65, 88, 118, 173
   Albany, 113, 124–126, 204
   Buffalo, 113, 204, 210
      St. James Hall, 210
   Mechanicsville, 124–126
   New York, 56, 59, 113, 118, 121, 124–126,
      129, 135, 165, 172, 173, 182, 192, 200,
      201, 203, 204, 207, 208, 209
      City Hall, 124–126, 207
      Trinity Church, 207
   Westfield, 99
New York Temperance Society, 80
New York Twenty-Second Regimental Band,
   138
Niagara Falls, 95
Nicolay, John George, 108, 111, 112, 144
Nolin Creek, 1
North Carolina, 65, 98, 122, 141

Oak Ridge Cemetery, 218, 238, 239
   Old Vault, 238
Oates, Stephen B., 76
O'Connor, Andrew, 110
Offutt, Denton, 16, 17, 23, 24
Oglesby, Richard J., 78, 198
Ohio, 98, 118, 155, 160, 168, 170
   Cincinnati, 78, 82, 86, 88, 92, 96, 97, 113,
      204, 211
   Cleveland, 113, 175, 204
   Columbus, 40, 113, 204
   Dayton, 52
Ohio River, 5
O'Laughlin, Michael, 230
Oregon, 65, 70, 155
Our American Cousin, 191, 192

Paine, Lewis (see Powell, Lewis)
Parke-Bernet Gallerlies, 8
Pendleton, George H., 155
Pennsylvania, 88, 118, 155, 170
   Erie, 210
   Gettysburg, 145, 146
   Harrisburg, 113, 204
   Philadelphia, 60, 81, 83, 100, 113, 122, 151,
      160, 176–178, 204, 206
      Independence Hall, 206
   Pittsburgh, 113, 204
   Reading, 171

Pennypacker, Samuel, 100
Periodicals
   Century Magazine, 111, 112
   Godey's Lady's Book, 144
   Harper's Weekly, 122, 123, 143, 155, 208
   Punch, 191
Petersburg and Weldon Railroad, 164
Petersen, William, 193, 197
Phillips Exeter Academy, 127, 128
Pierce, Franklin, 100
Pinkerton, Allan, 140
Polk, James K., 33
Pope, John Russell, 1
portraits, 60, 100, 149, 150, 188
   First Reading of the Emancipation Procla-
      mation, 149, 150
Powell, Lewis Thornton, 199, 230–234, 236,
   237
Pullman Company, 127, 128

Rathbone, Henry Riggs, 193–195
Rauch, E. H., 171
Rauch, W. H., 171
Rawleigh, T. W., 43
Raymond, Henry J., 70
Reed, John M., 60
Rehm, Charles, 135
Remington, John E., 8
Republican party, 64, 67, 69, 73, 80, 118, 141
   1858 Illinois State Convention, 39
   1860 Illinois State Convention, 78
   1860 National Convention, 30, 56–58, 66, 70
   1864 National Convention, 155
   presidential candidates, 39, 59, 65, 175
Rhode Island, 56, 64, 65, 88
Rickey, Mallory, 86, 88, 92, 96, 97, 98
Riney, Zachariah, 1
Rock River, 22
Roosevelt, Franklin D., 144
Roosevelt, Theodore, 1, 41
Root, George Frederick, 134
Rubins, David K., 9
Rutledge, Ann, 31

Saint-Gaudens, Augustus, 239
Sangamon Circuit Court, 27, 31
Sangamon River, 16, 17
Satin & Paper Badge Depot, 83
Saunders, William, 145
Scott, Dred, 92
Scripps, John Locke, 5, 16, 76
Sculpture, 9, 14–16, 18, 19, 21, 22, 26, 37, 42,
   44, 110
   Abraham Lincoln on the Prairie, 20
   And Now He Belongs to the Ages, 240
   Illinois 1830–1861, 12
   Indiana 1816–1830, 11
   Kentucky 1809–1816, 10
   Lincoln and Douglas in Debate, 41
   Lincoln the Circuit Rider, 18
   Lincoln the Debater, 43
   Lincoln the Lawyer, 36
   Lincoln the Ranger, 18
   Washington 1861–1865, 13
secession, 105, 115, 121
Seward, Augustus, 234
Seward, Frederick, 234
Seward, William Henry, 56, 70, 90, 118, 119,
   144, 158, 199, 234
Seymour, Horatio, 174
Shaw, William, 87
Shearman & Hart, 135
Shenandoah Valley, 139, 170
Shepherd, N. H., 32
Sheridan, Philip Henry, 155, 170
Sherman, William T., 155
Shiloh Cemetery, 106, 107

Siebert, M. W., 165
Sinclair, Thomas, 81
Sinking Spring, 1, 2, 10
slavery, 1, 39, 40, 42, 58, 59, 65, 86, 87, 105,
    115, 141, 142, 155, 159, 165
Smith, Caleb Blood, 118, 119
Smith, Carleton, 20
South Carolina, 65, 98, 105, 141
    Charleston, 65, 122, 123
    Columbia, 105
Spangler, Edman, 230
Speed, James, 119, 198
Speed, Joshua, 12, 31, 119
Stanton, Edwin McMasters, 118, 122, 131,
    132, 143, 158, 198, 204, 219, 240
Starkweather, L. B., 166
Statue of Freedom, 116
Strong, Sylvester, 47
Strong, T. W., 121
Stuart, John Todd, 12, 16, 27
Studebaker, Peter E., 6
Sumner, Charles, 173
Surratt, John H., 202, 230–231
Surratt, Mary E., 199, 230, 232–234, 236, 237
Swaney, James ("—— Sweeney"), 5
Swett, Leonard, 56

Taft, Lorado Zadoc, 36, 44, 239
Taft, William Howard, 1
Taylor, James, 5
Taylor, Tom, 191
Taylor, Zachary, 100
Tennessee, 59, 64, 98, 122, 141, 155
Texas, 65, 105
Thanksgiving, 144
Thomson, William Judkins, 51
Tilton, Lucius, 71
Todd, Elizabeth (Mrs. Ninian Edwards), 71
Todd, Frances (Mrs. William Wallace), 101
Todd, Lockwood, 130
Todd, Mary, see Lincoln, Mary Todd

Tolpo, Lily, 41
Tompkins, C. H., 230
Torrey, Fred M., 18, 239
Townsend, George Alfred, 198

Union, 13, 59, 62, 65, 105, 115, 121, 124–126,
    136, 137, 155, 159, 161–163, 165, 176,
    178, 203
Union League, 176–178
Union Republican party, 155, 167, 168, 170,
    173, 174, 175
United States Army, 139, 145, 190
United States Capitol building, 116, 184, 204,
    216
United States Constitution, 105, 172
    Thirteenth Amendment, 141
United States Government
    Congress, 27, 28, 32, 34
    Department of Agriculture, 145
    House of Representatives, 12, 27, 31, 33, 63,
        141
    Senate, 39, 40, 63, 141
    Supreme Court, 92
    War Department, 202
United States National Park Service, 72
Unites States Patent Office, 187
United States Secret Service, 140
University of Illinois, 36
    College of Law, 44
Usher, John Palmer, 119, 198

Vaas, A. J., 124–126
Vallandigham, Clement Laird, 160, 163, 170,
    173
Van den Bergen, Albert L., 26
Vermilion Circuit Court, 38
Vermont, 62, 88
    Brattleboro, 239
    Manchester, 127, 128
Vestuto, Antonio, 19
Virginia, 59, 64, 122, 127, 128, 141

Alexandria, 124–126
    Marshall House, 124–126
City Point, 13
Front Royal, 203, 235
Richmond, 139, 164, 170, 219
Winchester, 155
Volch, Adalbert John, 142
Von Schneidau, Polycarp, 48

Wabash River, 16
Walker, Lewis E., 182
Walker, Nellie V., 16
Wallace, Lew, 230
Wallace, William, 101
Warren, Henry F., 189
Washington, D.C., 16, 31, 60, 61, 99, 106, 108,
    110–113, 118, 124–126, 129, 130, 133,
    176, 191, 193, 197–199, 203, 204, 211,
    232, 233, 235
    Capitol Prison, 230, 236
    Pennsylvania Avenue, 204
Washington, George, 204
Webb, James Watson, 70, 90
Weeks, Alonzo, 119
Weik, Jesse W., 31
Weinman, Adolph A., 3, 239
Welles, Gideon C., 118, 119, 158, 198
Wenderoth and Taylor, 151
Whig party, 19, 33, 64
Whipple, John Adams, 71
White House, 94, 101, 111, 112, 117, 131, 146,
    149–151, 157, 178, 189, 240
    East Room, 124–126, 204
Wide Awakes, 73, 85, 94
Wigwam, 56, 57, 66, 78
Wilson, Woodrow, 1
Winchester, Stephen S., 40
Wisconsin, 98
Wood, Fernando, 173

Young, J. W., 100